THE GARDEN
OF SECRETS

HOPE AND HEALING

by Dr. Rosilda Alves DePina James

THE GARDEN OF SECRETS

HOPE AND HEALING

The author has checked with sources believed to be reliable in her efforts to provide information that is complete and generally in accord with the standards of practice that are accepted at the time of publication. However, in the view of human error, the author warrants that the information contained herein is in every respect accurate or complete, and is not responsible for any errors or omissions or the results obtained from the use of such information. Readers are encouraged to confirm the information contained in this book with other sources.

Give feedback on the book at: dr.rosildaj@gmail.com

www.rosildajames.com

Cover art by: Areana Amado, Adilson Amado, and Admilson Amado

First Edition

Printed in the U.S.A

This book is dedicated to my husband Duane,

and my children, Alexa and Ethan, who inspire me.

- TABLE OF CONTENTS -

IT TAKES A VILLAGE

First, I want to thank God for directing the writing of this book by providing amazing people with the professional knowledge, talent and support that I needed. I would like to thank my husband Duane James for his support (and editing), and our two amazing children, Alexa and Ethan, who fill us with hope. I thank my extended family for their support. Overall, I am grateful for both the positive and painful experiences that have given birth to this book.

I would like to thank Mrs. Sandra Montrond-Gomes and Mr. Joao Gomes, Mrs. Marise Lopes, Dr. Annette Chen, Miss. Patricia Ferreira, Mr. Jose Fonseca, Mrs. Arminda Fonseca, Miss. Shannon Rucker, Dr. Becky Pizer, and   Dr. Paul Gaiser for providing amazing feedback.

I also want to thank the three amazing artists, *meu sobrinhos*, who designed the book cover: Areana Amado, Adilson Amado, and Admilson Amado.

I offer a heartfelt thanks to the women of the 2016 Conference *Poderoza: International Conference on Cabo Verdean Women* hosted at Providence College in Providence, RI. Your love and support instill a new hope in us that it is time to address this issue in our community. I was so moved by the strength and development displayed by our women during this historic event.

Special thanks to Dr. Aminah Fernandes Pilgrim for her guidance, support, encouragement and editing. Heartfelt thanks for your friendship.

A Child

Oh God my soul is dying
Fighting spirit in paralyzed body
Crying heart in tearless eyes
Screaming voice in throat without words
Struggling to fight as hope disappears
Invasion, violation, destruction consumes
Dreams shattered,
Frightened child remained.

DEAR READER:

If you have been sexually abused, you are not alone. In the United States, one out of three girls and one out of seven boys are sexually abused by the time they reach the age of eighteen (Bass & Davis, 1998, p. 20).

Incest occurs in all cultures and classes and it leaves destructive and lifelong consequences. It is difficult to deal with because it is a family member doing the harm, and difficulty arises around the dilemma of having to choose to help one family member and punish another. However, it is time that we acknowledge this silent cancer eating many of the souls of girls and boys in Unites States, Cabo Verde, its Diaspora, and in global communities for multiple generations.

This book will focus on the Cabo Verdean community because whereas most cultures are able to talk about it and have understood its detrimental effects, much of our Cabo Verdean population—particularly the most rural, impoverished and less educated areas—remains in denial. Many often make excuses, and the general population often chooses to minimize its impact. This denial is due to the patriarchal nature of Cabo Verdean society, where male privilege dominates and excuses are made for negative male behaviors, or in some cases female behaviors. Most Cabo Verdean children are expected to obey and respect adults and remain silent. With this dynamic, when incest occurs the children feel alone, scared, confused and usually remain quiet – unable to voice their pain.

The time has long passed to change the current status, to go from protecting the perpetrator, to nurturing, protecting and loving the victim(s) in order to prevent further destruction of our children's spirits. Although the focus of this book is on females, most information provided can be applicable to male victims as well. Incest among boys is prominent in all cultures and classes and is also present in the Cabo Verdean community. I want to acknowledge their pain and suffering. The focus of the book is on one particular culture, but it is applicable to all collectivist cultures.

It should be acknowledged that I am a survivor of sexual abuse and a witness of repeated incidents of incest within our community that have been dismissed, ignored and denied. My story began similar to many others being violated by family members who were supposed to provide protection and nurturance. I, like you, was not equipped to face and deal with this violation that causes so much pain and leaves lasting scars. I was faced with confusion, fear, and anger at having many protectors become my torturers with no one to shield me or acknowledge my reality. I tried my best as any child to understand and survive the daily intrusions. In order to cope with the pain, I retreated to a fantasy world where I was powerful and able to punish the molesters and had a fantastic time plotting and imagining ways for them to pay. Secondly, I had an unfailing suicide plan that I would consider a few times a week as an option, but knew I would never take my life due to the pain it would cause my maternal grandmother. Thirdly, I spent time praying for God to provide a way out or to take me. My faith in God provided me with hope of being free from the abuse one day. This book is grounded in a Christian perspective since it is my own faith. However, you can apply any faith base that applies to you.

I decided at the age of 24 that for my mental health I needed to leave the comfort and pain of my family home to find safety and healing. I can honestly say that after substantial psychotherapy and spiritual growth, I am a happy, whole, caring person not carrying the shackles of shame and guilt that were never mine. I am in a loving marital relationship and I am a happy mother of two beautiful children.

I found peace and became an advocate for those whose voice and innocence was robbed. My journey to healing was long and painful, but the results were worth the pain.

With this book, my hope is to foster a dialogue rarely held in the Cabo Verdean community and to provide much needed professional information. As survivors and supporters, we will be empowered and courageous, and become allies for our abused and non-abused children. We will take the necessary steps to protect our children from future incidents of incest. We have a responsibility to fight for the safety of all children. My greatest desire is that this book will serve the goal of creating a safe world for children where trauma, assault and abuse are addressed and recognized as the destructive forces they are. They not only destroy innocence and shatter hope, but impact individuals' physical, spiritual and mental health as well. This book will provide the necessary information needed to begin to address these issues within the Cabo Verdean communities.

I speak to the heart of all the victims who have yet to share their stories or are unable to disclose due to their own individual reasons, which could be emotional, financial or survival based. I hope and pray that God (or your higher power) awakens in you the courage to transform your life to no longer be a victim. Your body and spirit can be renewed, and you can be free from the pain you have been carrying in silence. We have to create a culture where girls and boys feel safe to share their stories in the security of love and protection.

This book also speaks to the parents, the extended family, and members of the community by providing alternative and effective tools needed to facilitate support for boys and girls. The perpetrators are also provided with guidance to seek help and be accountable.

A caution for the victims: this book may trigger old, recent, or ignored feelings and if this occurs it may be good to seek professional help or call a help hotline for suggestions and support. Below are some telephone numbers to use to call for help.

National Sexual Assault Hotline:	1-800-656-HOPE
National Suicide Prevention Hotline:	1-800-273-TALK
National Center for Missing and Exploited Children:	1-800-THE-LOST
National Child Abuse Hotline:	1-800-422-4453
National Domestic Violence Hotline:	1-800-799-7233 or 1-800-787-3224 (TTY)

Girls and Boys (Survivors): Thank you for surviving this intrusion into your body, soul, and mind. I am so very sorry for all the ways in which you were betrayed and harmed by those who claimed to love and protect you. I am sorry you had to endure it alone. I pray you find your inner strength and you will be amazed how different life will be when your past no longer holds you hostage.

Being a survivor means you made it against all odds and that you are resilient, strong and ready to face the world. No more secrets, no more protecting their shame. It's time to be free of all past shame and blame. You are blameless, you are pure, you are beautiful and you are strong. Let the shackles of the past unbind you and see yourself through your creator's eyes.

My hope is that as you read this book it provides hope and insight. I hope it helps you to seek alternatives and gives you the courage to take those steps, as painful as it may be to free yourself. I hope it helps you to realize you are not alone and eases some of your suffering.

THE SERENITY PRAYER

God grant me the serenity
to accept the things I cannot change;
courage to change the things I can;
and wisdom to know the difference.

Living one day at a time;
enjoying one moment at a time;
accepting hardships as the pathway to peace;
taking, as He did, this sinful world
as it is, not as I would have it;
trusting that He will make all things right
if I surrender to His Will;
that I may be reasonably happy in this life
and supremely happy with Him
forever in the next. Amen.

By: Reinhold Niebuhr (1892-1971)

CHAPTER 1

HISTORY OF CABO VERDE

HOUSE OF PAIN
House of secrets and shame
House of love and pain
Infested with nightmares
Flooded with bleeding tears
Of confusion and fear
Brutally violated by love
Innocence sacrificed

"So do not fear, for I am with you; do not be dismayed, for I am your God. I will strengthen you and help you; I will uphold you with my righteous right hand."

— Isaiah 41:10

Our culture has a rich tradition of communicating hopes, dreams, and conflict through music and stories. We are a happy, helpful and hopeful community with a resiliency to cope. We have an ability to solve seemingly insurmountable problems. So why are we not unequivocally supportive to many of the innocent children being victimized through sexual abuse? Incest may be the most difficult type of abuse to endure because your loved one/family member and presumed protector becomes your abuser. Like all cultures, that of Cabo Verde is not immune to incest.

CABO VERDE HISTORY
According to local lore, "when God was satisfied with Creation, and brushed his hands together, the crumbs that fell unnoticed from his fingers into the sea formed Cabo Verde" (Irwin, 1998, p. 4). Cabo Verde consists of ten islands that are located off the coast of West Africa in the Atlantic Ocean. The islands are Sal, Sao Vicente, Sao Niculao, Santo Antao, Boa Vista, Santa Luzia, Maio, Santiago,

Fogo and Brava. When discovered around 1460 by sailors flying the flag of Portugal, the islands were thought to be uninhabited. Soon thereafter, the Portuguese established a population in the island composed of European settlers and Africans brought in from the African mainland primarily as slaves (Greenfield, 1976, p. 9). As a plantation society developed, the population evolved as a mixture of Africans and Europeans (including Jews) from the Iberian Peninsula; there is evidence of South Asian and Indian. Different races and cultures forming a unique identity as Cabo Verdeans, "a group of proud, hardworking, God fearing, loving, peaceful, generous and hospitable people" (Greenfield, 1976, p. 5).

Although located in the Atlantic Ocean, the islands are an extension of the North African desert. They are extremely arid and suffer from periodic drought. In the years with no rain, severe hardship befalls the residents. Many die of a combination of disease, starvation and dehydration, while countless others suffer (Monteiro, 1997, p. 30).

In 1747, the islands were hit with the first of the many droughts that have plagued them ever since, with an average interval of five years. The situation was made worse by deforestation and overgrazing, which destroyed the ground vegetation that provided moisture. Three major droughts in the 18th and 19th centuries resulted in well over 100,000 people starving to death.

IMMIGRATION TO THE UNITED STATES

As Joao Resendes-Santos documented, the first official record showed Cabo Verdeans immigrating to the USA in the mid-1700s (Halter 1993). Prior to independence in 1975, there were three great waves of outmigration; the first outmigration from the Portuguese colony was 1900-1926 was destined primary to the USA. The second wave, 1927-1945, was primarily toward Latin America and Africa while the third wave during 1945-1973 went to Europe.

According to Dr. Aminah Pilgrim's research, the first significant group of

Cabo Verdean immigrants to the USA came immediately after the U.S. era of reconstruction in the mid-19th century (1850s). These years have been characterized as some of the lowest and darkest within U.S. African American history due to the "Jim Crow" system of sharecropping and racial segregation. She shared the Cabo Verdean struggles within the USA during this time.

In the eighteenth and nineteenth centuries, American whaling ships stopped regularly in the islands. The whalers took on island natives to complete their crews. After several years at sea, the ships would return to their home ports in New England, often with their Cabo Verdean and other islander crewmen aboard. Some chose to stay, in the belief that America might offer them a better opportunity than their native islands. In time, small Cabo Verde 'colonies' were added to the racially and ethnically diverse and still growing cities of New England such as New Bedford, Massachusetts, Providence, and Rhode Island (Halter, 1985, p. 20). In this way, they joined the stream of immigrants coming to the shores of the United States in the late nineteenth and early twentieth centuries. Like other immigrants, they too were faced with the task of making a place for themselves in their adopted country (Halter, 1985, p. 12).

For almost a century, the establishment of a distinct social identity within the American society was not deemed necessary. This was the result of a unique development that enabled members of the Cabo Verde colony in New England to interact with and to relate primarily to other Cabo Verdeans, mostly outside the continental United States (Halter, 1985, p. 35).

As a result, their social world remained Cabo Verdean separated by oceans, but now connected by their ships. It would not be an exaggeration to say that New England and the Cabo Verdean Islands were in fact the geographical extremes of a single socio-economic universe (Halter, 1985, p. 43). Within that universe, the spoken language was *Kriolu*. Their hopes and aspirations were Cabo Verdean as was the institutional support structure for their emotional life. Their emotional rewards were to be obtained not from America, its people or institutions, but from other geographically dispersed Cabo Verdeans. Consequently, New England Cabo Verdeans had little interest in what their non-Cabo Verdean neighbors thought about them (Halter, 1985). Post 1930's (United States era of the Great Depression) and following the wartime trends in industrial growth, U.S. based Cabo Verdeans began settling in various small towns in southeastern Massachusetts, Connecticut and Rhode Island (and later on in places such as Ohio and Pennsylvania), where they would begin to move into factory jobs and public works day labor. The more recent waves of migrants—including myself and many of you reading this book—who immigrated in the 1980's, 1990's, and in the 2000's would settle in larger numbers in cities such as Brockton and Boston, MA, Pawtucket, RI and Newark, NJ. Patterns of cultural preservation and strong Diaspora (transnational) networks continued and still continue today.

ETHNIC IDENTITY

According to Aisling Irwin (1998), the faces of Cabo Verde are numerous: "blue eyes gazing out from above a brown cheek; green eyes below the tight curls of black hair with a wisp of blonde; Chinese eyes set in a black face. Race in Cabo Verde is not just Portugal mingled with the rivers of Guinea but also Italy and drops of Lebanon, China, Morocco and more. Pirates, sailors and merchants from Spain, France, England, Holland, Brazil, and America deposited their genes here. Senegambians, Mandingos and Fulas gave variety to the African blood that arrived in the forms of slaves. Cabo Verde has its own identity in an exciting synthesis. The Cabo Verdean people have their own history, the result of a unique combination of social and natural forces" (Irwin, 1998 p. 28).

CULTURAL CONNECTEDNESS

While there are more than a million people in the world who call themselves Cabo Verdeans, only about 300,000 people actually live on the islands. Most have found homes in Europe and the United States, often leaving loved ones and family members behind. They are isolated from the rest of the world, from their compatriots overseas, and even isolated by stretches of sea from their own countrymen and other islands (Monteiro, 1997, p. 22). However, what they lack in material wealth they compensate for in cultural richness. The people are mostly Creoles or Mestiços, descended from a mix of West African slaves and Portuguese colonists. The majority of the population speaks *Kriolu*, a language that blends antiquated Portuguese with West African language (Irwin, 1998, p. 5-10). The official language is Portuguese. It is used in school, for official functions, and for all written communication.

Cabo Verdeans have developed a sense of pensive longing that permeates their cultural expression. There is even a word that has come to describe this emotional state, one that has been immortalized in literature and songs and has come to define their character, "*sodade (or sodadi)*." Sodade suggests a sentiment of nostalgia, yearning for home and beloved ones. Sodade describes a bittersweet feeling that has no direct English translation, but one all Cabo Verdeans have felt at some time in their life (Irwin, 1998, p. 29). This sodade is a phenomenon that may be experienced by immigrants who leave loved ones behind to seek a better future. It is a constant painful longing to be with missed loved ones, missed places, and missed time.

Cabo Verde is a beautiful country with amazing, strong and enduring people. Arguably, most scholarly and popular writings about Cabo Verde, published in English, have focused on the unique geography and history of the islands, its mestiço culture and people, its Diaspora, and issues related to immigration, education, and politics. Within the Cabo Verdean community, many topics remain taboo and have yet to make their way fully into the literature. Thus, this book, "Garden of Secrets," seeks to disrupt this pattern and to begin a very necessary dialogue about a well-known, yet highly taboo subject—that of incest and sexual abuse of minors within the Cabo Verdean population.

When incest occurs, the community becomes paralyzed by a lack of understanding and awareness; victim blaming occurs despite good intentions. This book, based on my own doctoral research and thesis, aims to provide critical information needed to stop blaming the victims, to empower our beautiful and courageous people, to start holding perpetrators accountable, and to protect potential victims/current survivors from further harm. In this way, this book is written to strengthen individuals and families in our community, and to improve our community overall.

CHAPTER 2

CULTURAL SAMPLE: A VIEW OF SEXUAL ABUSE

Protectors
Grandma
Lovingly called me a liar and a whore
Mom
Supportively accused me of wanting it
Aunty
Protectively defended her brother
Father
Encouraging the birth of lies
Me
Abandoned and alone
Molester
Wrapped in family's love and support

" BE STRONG AND OF GOOD COURAGE, DO NOT FEAR NOR BE AFRAID OF THEM; FOR

THE LORD YOUR GOD, HE *IS* THE ONE WHO GOES WITH YOU.

HE WILL NOT LEAVE YOU NOR FORSAKE YOU."

– Deuteronomy 31:6

This chapter presents research completed for my doctoral program. The information provided here includes direct quotes from members of the Cabo Verdean community that authorized interviews for the project; the quotes reflect some widely held views on sexual abuse.

The study was specifically focused on Cabo Verdeans from the island of Fogo who reside in Massachusetts, and was completed in hopes that the research results would serve to educate and bring into popular awareness the effects of incest.

One of the major goals of the research was to investigate Cabo Verdean immigrants' attitudes toward incest, to determine whether sex between an adult and a child is perceived as exploitive or harmful to the child, and whether other influences such as blame attribution, poverty, gender (male) roles, religion, and collectivist views impact the Cabo Verdean definition of incest.

A sample of six Cabo Verdean families was recruited from the Massachusetts' Cabo Verdean population, specifically from the Boston and Brockton areas. Within each family, a female from each of three generations (grandmother, mother, and daughter) was selected. The participants' ages ranged from 18 to 99 years. The mean age for the grandmothers was 84, for the mothers 55, and for the daughters 21. None of the grandmothers had any formal education. They never attended school, not even preschool or elementary school; they worked at home and helped take care of their siblings. Two of the mothers had no formal education, three had below 6 years of formal education, and one had between 7 to 9 years of formal education. Four of the daughters had 10 to 12 years of formal education, and two had completed two years of college.

The interviews were conducted at the grandmothers' homes per their request. The participants denied the option of meeting in a neutral location to ensure confidentiality. The participants wanted the interview to take place in the kitchen or the living room with every one present. This radically differed from the procedure planned previously to ensure confidentiality. However, it illustrates the need for culturally sensitive modes of conducting research. The researcher asked that only one interviewee be present, unless previously interviewed, so that each participant spoke from her own experience.

The interview was conducted in *Kriolu* the native language of the participants and the researcher. Five of the daughters requested the interview in English since most of them were born in America.

The interviews used an open-ended stimuli to elicit responses that encouraged the participants to speak freely and spontaneously about their views on incest. The subjects were only informed that the topic was attitudes about incest and were not told that the material they provided would be analyzed for inherent themes related to incest attitudes. The intent of this design was to allow such themes to present themselves without prompting nor directing the subjects to provide such content. This design was intended to allow themes of blame attribution and generational differences or similarities to emerge, which were the focus of these interviews.

The steps in data analysis were a transcription and translation of the taped materials. The process of data analysis was a qualitative data reduction. A panel of four readers who were not aware of the hypothesis read the responses looking for themes according to a Grounded Theory approach. Caution to the reader: the following quotes and expressions are often very explicit and will most likely be triggers.

VIEWS OF THE MOLESTER

The grandmothers reported the following reasons as to why men sexually abuse girls:

- He took her assuming she was his woman.

- He was drunk.

- It's a temptation that grabs a man and he has to do it.

- A man in his right mind will not do it.

- In America, the drugs a man uses can destroy his common sense.

- He's gone crazy.

- That man is wrong, he has no head.

- Maybe he is drunk and out of his mind, and if he's not, what can one do?

- He is also family.

- You pray for courage to live and not have hatred in your heart and keep quiet

- He was not on his right mind.

- He should not do that.

- He should have known better.

- He could go to another woman, and if that did not work, he could go to an animal.

- If he wanted a virgin, he could go to a chicken for there is no reason for him to look at his daughter.

- Petroleum and matches don't mix.

- You can't give a wolf meat to guard.
- The man deserves to be killed. It happens a lot in our people.
- He's gone crazy.

The mothers reported the following reasons:

- That is wrong.
- The father is wrong.
- He could go to another woman.
- He could go to an animal, a chicken or a cow.
- He should be killed.
- His dick should be cut and forced fed to him.
- If anyone tried that on my daughter, I would kill them myself.
- Could be a man who drinks and loses control and has no idea what he is doing.
- That man should be condemned and so should the girl.
- That is a huge crime.
- It is the most dirty thing to happen.
- I condemn the father.
- He should be arrested.
- It's OK for men to be with young girls since it boosts their status and they tell jokes about it.
- It is glorified and seen as socially appropriate.
- I would send him to jail or kill him myself, but most Cabo Verdeans would blame the girl and protect the man.

The daughters reported the following reasons:

- The dad will not be touched.
- God forbid that a man's name be tarnished.
- That is for people to get together and kill him or send him to jail for life.
- The man should not have done this to her. This is her father and he has her mother.

- In Cabo Verde, they will hide it so as not to the lose family and people will not hear about it so the wife will not lose her husband.

- It is possible for the family to keep it covered for the rest of their lives and no one will know.

- In Cabo Verde, I don't think he will go to jail but in U.S. he could go to jail if it's shared outside the home ... it is kept between those who know in the family. Sometimes other people living in the house won't know,

- I don't think fear of jail will let them share it with a priest.

- Nasty.

- The guy is sick.

- The man should know better.

- It's the father, the adult, who did something to her.

VIEWS OF THE VICTIM(S)

The grandmothers reported the following views about how the family and community would handle the girl and the situation:

- The mother will hide it and say the girl should have told her.

- Keep it a secret.

- There's nothing one can do, you keep quiet.

- In the family, everything is kept quiet and it happens a lot.

- Maybe she wanted it to happen.

- She brought much shame to the family.

- She should know it is wrong.

- The mother will abandon the child.

- The child is to blame and since she did not say anything she liked and wanted it.

- The girl will stay home and no one will find out.

- He leaves his wife on the bed and goes to sleep with his daughter and no one complains.

- If it's me, I will keep the girl at home and kick him out.

- She is not at fault. Kids are like animals; they don't yet have the morals and judgement to know the differences.

The mothers reported the following views:

- The girl has no idea what she is doing.

- The girl is not to blame.

- The culture would like this kept quiet.

- Most Cabo Verdean moms would blame the daughter and have her keep quiet.

- God forbid a man's name be tarnished.

- The mother would let go of both husband and daughter.

- Lots of times the girl will be blamed for not saying something sooner.

- The 16-year-old girl is old enough to know the difference between right and wrong.

- The worst is the 6-year-olds because they are too young. The girl has no idea what she is doing.

The daughters reported the following views:

- That is sick. The girl does not know what she is doing.

- The community will look at her as if she is the one at fault. They will talk hush-hush and openly talk about her that she is a bitch, she wanted to do it. They would think she asked for it.

- The mother will blame the child; it does not matter if she is 17 or a 1-year-old.

- The mother will preserve her husband and take his side.

- The mother will find ways to turn the situation around and blame the child ... it is sick, but it is true.

- She will be treated as if this was her fault and that she should not have done it.

- Most mothers will act as if nothing is wrong.

- She will try to ignore it and not give an opinion to keep family together and quiet.

- She will sympathize with the daughter in private and in public she will support her husband.

- She did not consent.

- The child does not know any better.

- People will think she is a bitch.

- The community may look at her as being disgusting and degrading while in reality it is he who is degrading.

- The mother will blame the 16-year-old and make the 6-year-old believe she did something wrong or make her say it did not happen.

- She will tell her if you tell, I will hit you or promise her toys to keep quiet ... mom will definitely stay and support her husband.

SEX EDUCATION AT HOME

The grandmothers had the following responses:

- No one talked to us about these things.

- They spoke in codes that no one could understand.

- Girls are not allowed to go to school so they will not be able to write to boys.

- We were told not to be with boys and that boys are no good; stay away.

- There was no talking about intercourse.

- When I wash my kids I check them.

- I check their vagina to make sure they are OK in there because it is the parents' right and I tell them you don't want to be ashamed when you get to your house. What are you going to say? You were born with it so where is it (hymen)?

- In school, kids learn it and we as parents go to school and talk to teachers that they should not teach our kids those things.

The mothers had the following responses:

- This was never discussed. It would be disrespectful.

- It was disrespectful to talk about sex.

- This was not a topic of discussion in our home.

- The daughters had the following responses:

- It was never talked about in my home.

- It was never discussed.

- That was never talked about at home.

- Anything related to sex was considered disrespectful to talk about openly.

- We were never told anything.

- We never learned about our menstrual cycle.

- Mom never talked about it.

- My mother told me this is how you do things.

- She told me about condoms and things like that.

- They did not want you to learn anything about sex or have emotions toward boys. I wish my mother had talked to me about it.

- It's kind of embarrassing learning it at school with your friends.

- To have a teacher tell you it's kind of weird.

- It's a good way for parents to open communication at home so when kids go to school it may not be shocking.

CHILDREN'S RELATIONSHIPS TO ADULTS

The grandmothers had the following responses:

- We were never in the middle of adults.

- When people came to visit, our parents would give us a look and we knew to leave the room.

- Kids get their blessings when adults arrive and then they leave the room.

- Kids should not be in the middle of adults.

- They should listen to adults without talking back.

- The adults would just look at us and we would leave the room.

- Kids were never in the middle of adults.

- They were outside playing, not like now where the kids are in the middle of adults; no respect.

The mothers had the following responses:

- Mother will just lift her head and we knew it's time to leave and go outside.

- We were never in the middle of adults.

- If we did not listen, we would be in trouble.

- We would get a beating.

- I got beaten a lot because I was not good at staying where the kids were supposed to be; children are not heard in the family.

- Kids had a fear of parents.

- The kids had an oppressed life, not like now.

- We were scared of being hit.

The daughters had the following responses:

- They were out of adults' way.

- We were never involved in family discussions.

- You are children, you have no say.

- It was hard for both parents and kids to understand each other.

- It was a struggle and difficult to understand what parents expected from us.

- When a guest arrived, we knew not to be present.

- Boys did what they wanted because they are men.

- Girls stayed home because they could come home pregnant.

- We did not talk when adults were talking and we left the room when adults were together.

- Mom will wink at us and that meant that we are doing something wrong. If she does the wink more than once, we will expect a beating.

- She will not hit us in front of people or talk to us loud. If we don't see the wink, she will pinch us.

- We were not allowed to be part of important family discussions.

- Our job was to play and have fun, go to school and worry about nothing.

- When adults are around, the kids are not allowed.
- We were by ourselves most of the time.
- We were not allowed to be in adult conversations or in adult places.
- We did what adults told us to do.
- In Cabo Verde, it is stricter.
- Here, kids have more leeway and you can express yourself.

WHEN DID YOU LEARN ABOUT SEX

The grandmothers had the following responses:

- I was very innocent.
- I learned when I went with a man when I was 19 years old.
- No one told me.
- That was not talked about.
- I learned it from my husband.
- I was 20 when I went with a man.
- I was never told anything.
- Now, kids know more in the U.S.
- They listen to older people, they watch TV, and they learn it in school.
- I was 18 when I got pregnant, but I did not know how this was done until I was with him.

The mothers had the following responses:

- I became sexually active at 18 and had no idea what I was doing [2 respondents]
- I got married at 19. I was so scared when he became aroused. It was a scary night for me and I was not aware that this was how sex was.
- I learned at 18 when I left my parents' home with my boyfriend.

The daughters had the following responses:

- The nuns would talk to us about relationships with boys and the different diseases one could get.

- They talked about how one could protect themselves.

- TV, school. Now that I am 18, my mother talks to me, but not before.

- Friends and my mother told me this is how you do things. She told me about condoms and things like that.

- What I learned was from friends. A lot of girls had kids early because no one told them anything about how to have sex.

CULTURAL PERSPECTIVE

The grandmothers reported the following:

- He should not do it.

- When you hear that, it's the fault of parents because they should keep the girls separated from boys.

- There is a saying that petroleum and matches don't mix or you can't give a wolf meat to guard.

- A minor is just like a baby squash. It has no seed yet and it has to stay attached to its mom in order to grow big and produce seeds.

- If you cut it before its ready, it will not grow and mature, and if an adult talks or does everything in front of kids, they will keep it in their heads.

- Especially if they see parents do things, they will do it themselves because they think it's right.

- You can't sleep with your husband, just because you are married, in front of your kids. People who are born slow will die slow.

- Everyone who uses their head in front of their children, their kids will end up OK.

- I have no schooling, but I raised my kids in a way that you would think I am a doctor.

- You can't undress your girl in front of boys.

- Today, all kids are born with school. God gave me my head. I grew my kids well.

- I tell my kids a man who comes to you from another woman, don't accept him, because I know people who got a man's disease and died. She never got married because they got a disease with burning inside.

- Men are in control.

- When a woman leaves during the night with a man [without marriage] she is looked upon as damaged goods and no one will respect her.

- There were no churches in our time. We prayed at home ... family will not go to a priest [with incest].

- A girl will go with an older man because the government does not help by providing jobs for women to make a living.

The mothers reported the following:

- Men that go to Cabo Verde in search of a wife have been rejected by everyone in America.

- They go for 30 days and present well.

- They tried to sell me, but my mother said no because we were not that poor.

- They say if fathers are letting their girls out, it's not my fault if I took her. He should protect her.

- Cabo Verdean women cannot live an honorable life. The situation there makes it difficult for them.

- Cabo Verdean men visiting Cabo Verde leave multiple young girls behind with promises.

- They never look back or take care of the child left behind.

- Incest is against the law on earth and in heaven.

The daughters reported the following:

- Because of the poverty of the land, the woman needs a man to provide for her.

- The Cabo Verde community will look at her as if she is the one at fault.

- Women are as equal as men.

- God forbid a man's name be tarnished.

- The priest probably does it himself so he may take the man's side.

SECRECY

The grandmothers reported the following:

- On your wedding night, your godmother will give you pajamas to sleep in and early in the morning she will go to your room and get the pajamas to go wash and check if there is a blood stain and if you were a virgin.

- All the family and guests will be waiting to see if you are a virgin because this is the proof that will give the family honor. And if you are not a virgin the family will find out and if the man has class he may not send you back home.

- Some men will get you up and take you to your mother's home and leave you there.

- Some men will ask why you are not virgin and that is the time that most girls would say my dad's friend played with me or it was my uncle, my dad, my brother or whomever.

- In this moment, everything will be clarified. Some men will take you to your parents and knock on the door and say to your parents get up and take your dog.

- There is nothing one can do when incest is discovered.

- You keep quiet in the family. Everything is quiet.

- There is nothing you can do.

- You talk about not doing it again and keep things quiet in the family.

- I know someone who… both mother and daughter were pregnant at the same time by the dad. They gave birth and the mother raises both kids as her own and only a few people know.

- Everything is quiet.

- He leaves his wife on the bed and he goes and sleeps with his daughter and no one complains.

- The daughter marries a guy and she told him because she was having sexual problems and then the community became aware.

- There are those that will call the police.

- You keep quiet in the family, everything is kept quiet.

- Keep quiet, pray for courage to live and not have hatred in your heart.

- Whose mouth would open to tell a priest? It stays between the people who know.

- The mother will cry; there is nothing she can do or say.

- She can't go to court. No one will find out and the girl will stay home and no one will find out.

The mothers reported the following:

- This is something a family needs to resolve alone. It should not be spread because it can destroy the family name.

- The priest will advise the family not to let it happen again.

- If the public is aware of this, she will be tarnished for life. Men will say since your father took your hymen he owns you, I don't. That is why families keep it a secret. She may have a chance of finding a husband if no one knows.

- We take turns to tell a poem and it is a secret way to send messages to a boy that we like without telling them directly.

- Poetry is a way of communicating our feelings to boys since we were not allowed to be with them.

The daughters reported the following:

- Mom will act as if nothing is wrong [incest].

- She will ignore it and try not to give an opinion.

- It is kept between those who know in the family.

- Sometimes other people living in the house won't know.

- Mom may not blame anyone so things can keep going as they are without breaking up the family and keeping quiet.

- Cabo Verdeans like to keep secrets and they work hard to keep everything within the house.

- The priest will probably stay out of it for the sake of the community.

- He may try to keep it a secret and support an abortion or help cover it up.

- Cabo Verdeans are stuck in their way of covering things up.

- Our culture covers things up for the sake of the community or someone's reputation.

- There is a lot of covering up and presenting well.

- The mother will tell the [child] if you tell I will hit you or promise her toys to keep quiet.

- Mom will cover the whole thing up so people will not find out and she will definitely stay and support her husband.

- Anything related to sex is considered disrespectful to talk about openly.

- It is possible for the family to keep it covered for the rest of their lives and no one will know.

MEN'S POWER AND CONTROL

The grandmothers reported the following:

- She is dependent on a man.

- A man works and takes care of the family. If a woman tried to say anything, she would be hit.

- Women were beaten all the time with sticks, cooking woods, belts and rocks. They were often seen with black eyes.

- Women were severely beaten in Cabo Verde and in America.

- In Cabo Verde, women were hit by men when they were out of line.

- A man has to be in charge. If he hits her once, he will not do it again because she will learn.

- Chickens (women) have one nest. A rooster (man) will not lay in one nest.

The mothers reported the following:

- Women never had a say.

- It was always the man.

- In Cabo Verde, women were maids to their men.

- I remember being hit for hitting a boy without anyone asking me my reasons for hitting him.

- We were treated very differently.

- There were girls' jobs and boys' jobs.

- Girls stay home and learn from mom while dad goes to the field and teaches the boys.

- Boys had more freedom.

- They were allowed to stay out late and girls were not allowed to be out without an escort.

The daughters reported the following:

- Boys did what they wanted because they are men.

- Girls stay home because they can come home pregnant.

- Cabo Verde men are in control.

- They get up first, they speak first.

- The women are one step behind them.

- The wife makes no complaints or demands.

- She takes good care of him hoping he might spend the whole night.

- My brothers can go out and come late, but girls can't stay out late.

- In Cabo Verde, they think men are above women.

WOMEN'S POWERLESSNESS

The grandmothers reported the following:

- In our country, the women listen to all that men say.

- When the man says something, you will not answer.

- You will do all that the husband says.

- Women in America will not follow the rules of men.

- I still follow the rules of my husband. Not a lot of women are allowing men to rule.

- Here, women have taken roosters' roles and men have become the chickens.

- It's hard for men if they are not used to this. They will have hard time here. If you listen to your husband, everything will go well. He is the head of the house. If he is not allowed to rule the house, lots of things can go wrong.

- Here is not like Cabo Verde. There, men will leave and women stay home. Here, it's not like that.

- There, when a man leaves, the woman sits and waits until morning and when he gets home she takes care of him without raising her voice because if he notices she's unhappy he will hit her. Here, women will not accept that.

- In Cabo Verde, when a woman leaves, she is damaged goods and no one will respect her.

- A woman tries to find a better life for her kids. That is why she leaves one man who could be abusing her because of drinking and being lazy and unable to provide, and she finds someone who can provide.

- There is a saying my grandmother used to say that a woman who is a bitch does not exist. A scumbag of a man is what makes a bitch. By not treating her right, he forces her to go to another man. This saying stuck to my head and I tell other women this that if a man is not treating her well, she needs to find another.

- Women are patient.

- A woman has to suffer and remain if she is a good woman. Men can come and go, but women have to wait. Men are in charge, in control. She is dependent on a man.

- She looks for opportunity and security, and love may not be there.

- One learns to love someone who treats you well and you hate the one you love because they don't treat you well.

- Women will look for someone who has something to give...this is because of poverty. She is looking to better her situation.

- A good man will take care of you and treat your parents right and treat you like a wife.

- If the man is married, you can be with him, but with agreement of the wife.

- Back then women were for helping each other. I never fought for a man.

- The woman is looking to better her situation. Her parents would encourage her not to let the opportunity pass.

- When girls go somewhere, we give them someone to walk with. Girls (when they enter puberty) do not walk by themselves (escorted by another female who is older).

- Lots of kids went to their house early with older men. They came back with man's disease.

The mothers reported the following:

- A woman depends on a man to provide for her. She is interested in his money and the possibility of coming to America because of poverty.

- Girls are in search of a better life.

- The men in Cabo Verde are in charge, not like America where women have power.

- Women never had a say. It was always the men.

- Women were beaten in Cabo Verde and are still getting beaten if they try to get a little power.

- Cabo Verdean men in America continue with this thinking.

- Women miss work for weeks because they have black eyes.

The daughters reported the following:

- Women are as equal as men. I don't believe that a man is above a woman. A woman has her own mind and the right to express her feelings without a man controlling her.

- A woman depends on a man to treat her.

- Women in Cabo Verde are few who are with men for love. Women will try to be with a man who can provide even if he is abusive. At least he'll provide food because there women have to depend on men.

- It's true that women are beaten by men. There is nothing a woman can do.

- You just have to suffer quietly.

- Cabo Verde women have a price, just like a horse or a pig.

- Parents are the ones selling the girls to the highest bidder.

- In Cabo Verde, they think men are above women. The men are working, but the women stay home.

- Both should be equal.

- My mom told me how women were treated badly for anything.

- I believe Cabo Verde is set in a rigid way where the man makes all the decisions, not like here where women can work and have a say.

- In Cabo Verde, kids have their place and women have their own. Whatever decision needs to be made, the women have no say; it's all up to the man ... She can't judge a man. They are allowed to stay home, cook, clean, and take care of the kids.

- I see as women come to the U.S. and they establish themselves, they go to the work force and realize they are equal like the man. Like my mother, she goes to work like my stepfather. She has a say in what is done with the money. She may still have the mentality that a man has the power. However, she has a feeling that she is equal.

- I see many Cabo Verdean women still serving their men.

- When I am older, I definitely know that I am equal and that we are partners and I am not subservient to him. Most Cabo Verdeans who were raised here still don't want to get away from that thinking and that the man has to be on top.

- Their belief is so strong that they can't get away from it. It's their identity, it's who they are, and it's difficult to get away from that.

- If a man has position, you leave a young boy and go with him. He'll give you a better life.

- Women will try to be with a man who can provide even if he is abusive. At least, he'll provide food because there women have to depend on a man in Cabo Verde.

- Girls want to get with a man who is foreign and with money. Because of poverty in the island, they need a man to provide for them.

- In Cabo Verde, if he provides for me I would provide for him sexually so he can provide for me and my kids. When you are poverty stricken, options are limited.

- And you basically have no future. I think the choice is leaning towards sleeping with the old man. She is put in that position where she has to give herself up just so that she can have a chance at life.

SUMMARY OF RESEARCH

These painful quotes represent a small sample and should not be generalized. It has to be made clear that they cannot be generalized to represent the ten islands or even the island of Fogo where the participants originated. One needs to be mindful of the education levels and the rural locations of the participants' upbringing.

The objective of this study was to explore Cabo Verdean immigrants' attitudes towards incest. The research posed four questions: First, is there any blame attributed to Cabo Verdean incest survivors? Second, how does the Cabo Verdean culture handle sex education? Third, how does the Cabo Verdean culture view incest? Fourth, are there generational differences or similarities in attitudes toward incest?

The first research question investigated blame attribution.

Five out of six grandmothers interviewed had some form of excuse for why a man commits sexual abuse. Five grandmothers shared that the man could have been drunk, confused, insane, or not able to help himself as in "you can't give a wolf meat to guard." One grandmother stated that the man should be killed. Their view for the victim, with the exception of one, was that the girl is responsible; she wanted it since she did not report the abuse and the mother will side with the husband. However, one grandmother stated she would keep the girl and kick the husband out.

Five mothers stated that the man was wrong and should be incarcerated, killed or castrated. They also stated that it is difficult to blame men or damage their reputations. One mother reported that the man was drunk or had lost control. They shared that the girl had no idea what she was doing. However, the culture and most moms would blame the girl.

The daughters claimed that it was difficult to blame men in the culture and their good reputations were well preserved. However, they held the man responsible and shared that the girl is blameless, but that the culture and the mother would blame the girl and keep it quiet. The mother will remain with the husband. The girl will be negatively marked and called degrading names by the community and some mothers will get the child to lie in order to keep it quiet and preserve the father's reputation.

The second research question examined how Cabo Verdeans handle sex education.

All the grandmothers reported that there were no sex education discussions at home. Sex education at home was considered disrespectful and the girls were told to stay away from boys. The grandmothers agreed that as kids they were never allowed in the midst of adults. The grandmothers reported that they learned about sex when they became sexually active at 18, 19 and 20 years of age. They reported being innocent and unaware until then.

All the mothers reported that sex was not discussed at home and that it was considered disrespectful to talk about sex. They were not allowed in the midst of adults and that their parents would just lift their faces or wink at them and they knew to leave the room. They reported being beaten a lot when they refused to obey adults. The mothers learned about sex at 18 and 19 years when they were intimate with men. One woman stated that she was scared at her wedding night when her husband became aroused.

All the daughters reported that sex education was never discussed at home. Anything related to sex was considered disrespectful to talk about openly. They all reported that as kids they were not allowed in adult conversations or in family discussions and that children had no say in the family. They reported that boys were allowed to go out while girls could not because they may return pregnant. They reported learning about sex at school from friends, Sunday School and one daughter from her mother when she was 18 years old.

The third research question was the cultural view of incest.

The grandmothers reported that the incest is kept a secret within the family and there was nothing that could be done. The males in the community hold the power and control. Due to this power, several domestic violence incidents were never reported. On the other hand, they discussed the powerlessness of the women. Women listened to what men said and did not question their behavior or the number of sexual partners they had. This created an ideal situation for incest to occur. In addition, the secrecy implied lack of knowledge of the severe impact of incest. The cultural view is that it is kept quiet and that life goes on as if nothing had happened, and this increased the belief that it has minimum impact on the female.

For clarification, there are many powerful Cabo Verdean women who have questioned and pushed the system by advocating for changes and have made important impacts in shifting the paradigm.

The mothers also reported that men hold the power and control in the community, and that women are powerless and depend on men due to the poverty of the land. Women were severely beaten by the men and that it continues in America. Domestic violence continues to be an issue of concern that needs serious attention in the community.

The daughters believe that a woman and man should have equal power. However, they see that other women depend on the men to provide even if he is abusive. Most women find someone who can provide security not love. There was nothing women could do; they just have to suffer quietly because it has been going on for so long that it has become part of their identity. With this powerlessness continuing, it is difficult for a mother to protect her daughter given the amount of power males hold.

The fourth research question explored the generational differences and similarities.

The similarities among the participants were the consistency of power and control held by the males and the difficult situation a woman is in. She does not have a voice and is severely beaten if the shares her opinion. These put her in an oppressive position where she cannot protect her children. He dictates how things are and should be. The second consistent point was the lack of sexual education at home and the fact that it was disrespectful to talk openly about sex.

The differences presented were that grandmothers held the girl(s) responsible for the incest while most of the mothers and daughters held the man responsible and felt the girl was blameless. They also expressed the feeling or the assumption that the cultural power of blaming the girls was indestructible.

DISCUSSION

This research study hypothesized that a Cabo Verdean's attitude towards incest and child sexual abuse would be perceived as non-exploitive. The results confirmed that incest was non-exploitive, as viewed by the grandmothers and mothers. Most of them felt that life would continue as if nothing had happened. This view was culturally supported by the culture's power in silencing the victim and the power difference held by the men. However, from the daughters' responses, it is clear that they saw incest as exploitive, which may have to do with acculturation and their levels of education.

CULTURAL DIFFERENCES

Most of the participants view incest as non-exploitive with the exception of the daughters who were born in America or had become acculturated. This view of incest as non-exploitive could create great conflict within the American culture where they reside. Therefore, American professionals need to be educated as to the reasons this community views incest as non-exploitive. The families are not neglectful or unprotective. Rather, it is an adaptation formation to deal with these incidents as best they can. Denying incidents of incest is the best way they know how to "protect" the victim and community. They do not consider how incest affects the victims; rather, the priority is how it could impact the community both here in America and in Cabo Verde (or elsewhere in the Diaspora). If the molester is supporting family both in America and in Cabo Verde, disclosing incest would have a transnational economic effect. For instance, the family in Cabo Verde relies on assistance arriving from America and if the molester goes to jail there would be no one to care for the family in Cabo Verde or at home. In addition, the family name would be brought under scrutiny, which would cause the victim to lose her virtue and have no hope of a future. For these reasons and many more, the culture's best way of handling incest is to do nothing, but in private give the victim a word of encouragement; thus, both go on strong because they have a history of overcoming trauma.

American professionals that interact with individuals from Cabo Verde need to understand the Cabo Verdean culture and meaning behind their actions because what may appear as neglectful could be in reality a form of protection; i.e., saving the victim's virtue and preserving family/community subsistence. What could be seen as a lack of protection, in reality, could be a form of looking at the best interest of the community as a whole and at the impact to the family in Cabo Verde that relies on the molester for its survival.

It is clear that community members would wish that incest not occur. However, when it does, the community continues to function as if nothing has happened. The mother cannot afford to split the family and the family cannot afford to share this outside the community. In the most loving family, when incest occurred the best way to continue functioning is to pretend nothing has happened. The culture expects the mother to be loyal to her husband, which takes precedence over what Americans may see as not protecting a child. If the culture were to see incest as exploitive, then the systems in place would not be effective. As long as incest is seen as non-exploitive, the victims have no choice but to appear unaffected by incest and act as if nothing is wrong, which increases and intensifies the belief that it is non-exploitive.

It appears that illiteracy and poverty feed the cultural tradition of keeping incest a secret and other problems within the family. The lack of developed knowledge makes it impossible for the community to gain insight and have access to alternative options. In addition, the culture communicates values through storytelling, metaphors, and music, which to a degree relies heavily on past tradition and pays less value on present and future knowledge. This approach is true for the older generation. However, the new generation is getting educated and gaining knowledge while valuing oral tradition, but not relying on it alone.

This cultural tradition believes that a woman loses her self-respect and ability to marry if she is not a virgin. It is also known that in the past history, once a female reaches puberty, she needs to be accompanied by an adult to supervise her behavior and actions and to make sure her virtue remains intact. If she is not home by sunset and is unaccompanied, she will not be allowed to return home unless she can prove she was not with a man. If a woman becomes pregnant or moves in with a man out of wedlock, she is to leave her parents' home in the dark before they become aware of her disgrace, which is known as "Sai de Case" or going in the dark. Since she has brought shame to the family, her leaving at night symbolizes her respecting the family and acknowledging her error. While she is in hiding, if she sees a member of her family, especially a male, she is to show her respect by hiding. She will remain in hiding until the family forgives her and welcomes her back in the family. However, this view that is held in the island of Fogo has radically changed over the years.

The results support the cultural view of women being blamed, degraded, and shamed if her virginity is not intact when she gets married. This view could be another reason why incest is kept a secret so the female could have a chance at life and prevent the shame that comes with her inability to keep her virginity intact. Since the culture does not hold men responsible for a woman's virtue, the circumstances under which she loses her virginity are not considered. The reality is that she is not a virgin, and a stigma is connected to her for the rest of her life. Again, this view has changed with the new generation.

The daughters' views were radically different from the grandmothers and mothers, and one might assume that this difference causes conflict within the generations, which it does. However, when it comes to important decisions, the daughters' points of view are not seriously taken into account. The power lies with the men or the elderly women in the family. The cultural view values wisdom that comes from age rather than a daughter who holds a high scholastic degree. Furthermore, the culture will place more respect and value on a married daughter than on a single one with a doctoral degree. For these reasons, it appears difficult to change the view held by the culture.

31

In summary, the culture has a rich tradition of communicating hopes, dreams, and conflict through music. The music lyrics in the researcher's literature review clearly stated where power is located in the culture. There are incredible amounts of responsibility placed on girls to protect their virginity. In addition, the families and the victims' primary concerns are the financial hardship if the perpetrator's actions became known. The beloved priest Father Pio stated in an interview in 1999 that "Cabo Verdean Americans as a cultural group have a history of experiencing traumatic events. While these traumas are significant, many Cabo Verdeans seem to possess a resiliency to cope. Cabo Verdeans' valuing of religion and spirituality has its influence on their ability to solve seemingly insurmountable problems."

LIMITATIONS OF THE STUDY

The entire findings in this study must be considered within the context of several methodological and procedural limitations. The constraints affected the generalizability of the results to a larger population, and the problem with instrumentation may have affected the outcome of the study. This research is meant to be used as a guide to begin a dialogue and educate where limitations resides.

First, there was a plan for a consistent interview process. However, the reality was that most of the daughters requested that the interview be in English while the interviews with the grandmothers and mothers were in Cabo Verdean *Kriolu* since most, if not all, could not speak English.

The second concern was that the grandmothers requested that their daughters be present during the interview. With this request, the mothers were interviewed before their mothers (i.e., the grandmothers) since the questions were the same. The mothers periodically assisted their mothers in answering questions. This assistance could have changed the answer. However, I paid close attention and removed the responses that grandmothers did not change or clarify after her daughter's assistance. This modified process also demonstrated communal support.

The third concern was that the mothers wanted to be tested with several family members and friends present. There was an interview where the mother requested assistance from her family, and in order to get her response, all the family members were allowed to respond after the mother. In the middle of this interview, the mother yelled out the window for a friend to come in and join the interview. The friend also was answering questions. The only response that was used was the mother's. These interjections were clearly a cultural demonstration of communal focus rather than individual. They could have impacted the response of the mother or made it richer.

The fourth concern was in the translation of the responses from *Kriolu* to English and interview questions from English to *Kriolu* and back to English. For example, the translation of "intercourse" to the *Kriolu* language had to take a different form since it was disrespectful to talk about sex directly. It had to be stated using expressions such as "when you went with a man," "when making babies," or "when you went with a man for the first time." When the responses had to be translated into English, some items were not translatable and lost a lot of their meanings in the translation.

The fifth concern was the sampling size and formal education (or lack thereof) of participants. The sampling size (18 participants) was too small for generalizations. Furthermore, given the lack of formal education, many did not fully understand the implications of such research.

The sixth concern was that the sample consisted from people only from the island of Fogo. Therefore, the results cannot be generalized to people from all the ten islands. All the islands are uniquely different and will respond differently.

AREAS FOR FUTURE RESEARCH

The research study contributed to the limited information available on Cabo Verde, especially Cabo Verdean immigrants, and suggested the importance of continued research in this area. Such research should first attempt to duplicate this study with a higher statistical power in order to verify its validity. New variables should then be introduced, including effects of incest on the survivor both short term and long term.

Further research and education on the impact of incest on the survivor and on domestic violence would provide information necessary to educate the community on the seriousness of their effects. Considering the growth trend of Cabo Verdeans in this country, one needs to be able to understand the culture and its strengths and weaknesses. The implications of this research (or any such exploration of a similar Diaspora population) are critical since they offer an intervention that may be applied to any small, transnational, patriarchal, collectivist culture of immigrants in the U.S. which very well may have similar patterns and taboos (e.g., immigrants from Africa, India, Asia, Latin America, and other like communities). A lack of understanding would impinge on psychologists' ability to provide quality services to this community. Furthermore, this lack of knowledge might further exacerbate the misconceptions of the current needs of this population. Objective research studies in this area may help educate the community about the concerns and realities of the impact of incest.

I was honored to meet with these families and collect these rich views and the rest of the book will address the views by challenging some and educating on others.

CHAPTER 3

SEXUAL ABUSE

Betrayed
Betrayed by hands of love
Innocence shattered by my defender
House full of blind and deaf nurturers
Shame and secrecy prevail
Alone and secretly I bled
An imposter's smile dominates

"THE LORD IS MY ROCK, MY FORTRESS AND MY DELIVERER;
MY GOD IS MY ROCK, IN WHOM I TAKE REFUGE."
– Psalm 18:2

Children and individuals from ethnic groups such as Cabo Verde are especially vulnerable to child sexual abuse because they are less likely to report or seek help. It is crucial for Cabo Verdeans to understand the impact of incest and child sexual abuse because their children may be especially at risk for long term effects due to the cultural tendency to blame the victim and suppress disclosure of the abuse. The act of incest is considered a taboo in almost all cultures worldwide.

The U.S. Department of Health and Human Services' Children's Bureau's report "Child Maltreatment 2010" found that 9.2% of victimized children were sexually assaulted. Studies by David Finkelhor, Director of the Crimes Against Children Research Center, show that 1 in 5 girls and 1 in 20 boys is a victim of child sexual abuse. According to a 2003 National Institute of Justice report, 3 out of 4 adolescents who have been sexually assaulted were victimized by someone they knew well. A study conducted in 1986 found that 63% of women who had suffered sexual abuse by a family member also reported a rape or attempted rape after the age of 14. Recent studies in 2000, 2002, and 2005 have all concluded similar results.

According to the National Center of Child Abuse and Neglect (2010), in America, child sexual abuse is one of the most underreported forms of child maltreatment and one that often remains undetected. Short and long term effects of incest and sexual abuse are well documented. Mental health professionals and researchers have discovered that persons surviving sexual abuse experience low self-esteem, depression, impaired functioning, substance abuse disorder, anxiety disorder, personality disorder, sexual impairment and other impairments (Finkelhor & Hotaling, 1990, p. 35).

FACT SHEET from Parents For Megan's Law **The Statistics of Child Sexual Abuse** **According to National Association of Adult Survivors of Child Abuse.**
One in three girls and one in six boys are sexually abused before the age of 18.
1 in 6 boys is sexually abused before the age of 18.
One in 5 youth received a sexual approach or solicitation over the Internet in the past year.
The average age for first abuse is 9.9 years for boys and 9.6 years for girls.
Abuse typically occurs within a long-term, on-going relationship between the offender and victim, escalates over time and lasts an average of four years.
Many child sexual abuse victims never disclose their abuse to anyone. Less than 12% of child sexual abuse is reported to the police.
Children are most vulnerable between ages 7-13.
29% of all forcible rapes occurred when the victim was under 11 years old.
15% of sexual assault and rape victims are under the age of 12.
44% of sexual assault and rape victims are under age 18.
Children with disabilities are 4 to 10 times more vulnerable to sexual abuse than their non-disabled peers.
Nearly 30% of child sexual assault victims identified by child protective service agencies were between 4 and 7 years of age.

93% of juvenile sexual assault victims know their attacker, 34.2% of attack
ers were family members and 58.7% were acquaintances and only 7% of the
perpetrators were strangers to the victim.

Nearly 50% of all the victims of forcible sodomy, sexual assault with an object,
and forcible fondling are children under the age of 12.

60% of girls who had sex before the age of 15 were coerced by males averag-
ing 6 years their senior.

Women who experienced sexual abuse as a child are 2 to 3 times more likely
to be sexually assaulted later in life.

Like rape, child molestation is one of the most underreported crimes: only
1-10% are ever disclosed. Source: FBI Law Enforcement Bulletin.

Fabricated sexual abuse reports constitute only 1% to 4% of all reported cases.
Of these reports 75% are reported by adults. Children fabricate sexual abuse
less than 1% of the time.less than 1% of the time.

**IT IS ESTIMATED THAT THERE ARE 60 MILLION SURVIVORS OF
CHILDHOOD SEXUAL ABUSE IN AMERICA TODAY.**

According to the U.S. State Department's Cabo Verde 2013 Trafficking in
Persons Report:

"The Government of Cape Verde does not fully comply with the minimum for the elimination of trafficking; however, it is making significant
efforts to do so. The government investigated at least two cases involving
alleged child prostitution, an increase compared to its failure to investigate any cases of suspected human trafficking in the previous reporting
period. In addition, it began prosecution of three offenders in one case.
The Cape Verdean Institute for Children and Adolescents (ICCA), under
the Ministry of Youth, Employment, and Human Resources Development,
made concerted efforts to protect child victims of sexual abuse, including
children in prostitution, and to assist vulnerable children. Despite these
efforts, the government did not prosecute or convict any trafficking of-

fenders during the year. Furthermore, it did not make efforts to identify any trafficking victims or reduce the demand for commercial sex acts." Given that sexual abuse is present in all cultures and class, it appears that Cabo Verde is in its infancy regarding identifying and prosecuting perpetrators and supporting the victims.

DEFINITION OF INCEST

There is now an evolving definition of incest that takes into consideration the betrayal of trust and the power imbalance in these one-sided relationships. One such definition is: "the imposition of sexually inappropriate acts, or acts with sexual overtones ... by one or more persons who derive authority through ongoing emotional bonding with that child." (Blume, 1990, p. 4). This definition expands the traditional definition of incest to include sexual abuse by anyone who has authority or power over the child. This definition of incest includes as perpetrators: immediate/extended family members, babysitters, school teachers, scout masters, priests/ministers, etc. "Incest between an adult and a related child or adolescent is now recognized as the most prevalent form of child sexual abuse and as one with great potential for damage to the child". (Courtois, 1988, p. 12).

FORMS OF INCEST
TOUCHING

This form includes any touches that sexually gratifies a man. For example, when a man hugs a young girl too tightly or for too long in fun and everyone laughs and make statements like the following:

- He's crazy.
- He is so friendly.
- He is always playing.
- He is like that with all the girls.
- Such a friendly man.
- He is so nice.

A touch that appears innocent to the world, but leaves one feeling dirty and uncomfortable is a specialty of many males in the community. Touching body parts accidentally, but with a delay in removing the hand, may or may not lead to a sarcastic apology. Often at parties, you see the older males leaving their wives sitting while they dance with younger girls and this is sanctioned by the culture. Often, these substantially older men take girls to dance for sexual stimulation, which is achieved by holding the girls tight in "fun." The above touches, when done without the intent of sexual gratification, can be appropriate and be a way of demonstrating affection and connectedness of the community.

This description is not to say that all the men in our community behave in this manner. Like all cultures, there are many wonderful well-respected men who respect and do not objectify children nor abuse them. It is time for our honorable males to hold the child molesters accountable for abusing children.

Another example is the perpetrator becomes very friendly with girls in front of their parents and has them sit in his lap. He places a girl on top of his penis and she can feel his arousal and it appears no one notices. Or, sadly, the known abuser of the family will take a young girl to another room to play, give her a ride to the store, take her for a drive, and nothing is done. No one questions it. No one follows. No one protects. These are the areas that need focus and immediate changes.

What would happen if all mothers refused their minor children to dance with known child molesters and stopped them from making statements like "you will be my bride, you and I will marry?" And what if mothers would say "you cannot take my child to another room because I remember what you did to me." I wonder how this would make our girls feel. What if mothers stopped males from playing these suggestive sexual games with their daughters? What if we began to notice the harm in allowing them to play? The worst part is when we allow the perpetrators to behave this way in our presence. We disempower our girls and empower the males and then the innocent game between the two gradually increases to full penetration in private.

For example, as a young teen, I recall a 3-year-old girl playing around on the beach wearing only her diapers. There was a group of 50+ year old man playing cards and one man reached over and touched the little girl's nipples and said to the other man "look at that beauty, she will turn out nice." He again touched her, and I grabbed the girl and dressed her and told them that they were disgusting to be looking at a 3-year-old in that manner. One of the wives stood up and said "You make innocent games dirty. He was just playing with her." So I responded with a saying that is often expressed in our culture, " E na brincadera que macaco fode se mai." There is no direct English translation, but the idea is that a horrible behavior is excused with a light joke. I wonder about this saying and its origin given that it is so often used in our community.

LOOKS OR COMMENTS

The second and third form of incest can be a seductive look or a comment. I can say with some certainty that these have happened to most, if not all, girls in the community by substantially older males. Often, an older man shakes a girl's hand and simultaneously scratches the palm of her hand as an expression of sexual interest. Older men also make inappropriate, unwanted comments (most often in *Kriolu*) to teen girls like:

- I like your backyard.
- You look good (Sta Boa).
- When I do you, you will have to learn to walk again.
- Your breast is ripe, ready to be sucked.
- Nice ass, nice lips to be sucked.
- When will you let me do you.
- I will have to have you one of these days.
- You are ready for sex.
- If you don't give it to me, I will have to take it.

The sad point is that this behavior has become the norm and no one challenges these men. Because of their age and the cultural practice that dictates youth should respect their elders, girls feel fearful to say anything or see it as normal, and the males see no harm in what they are saying. The sexual look and suggestive expression are always present due to the objectification of females in the community due to the patriarchal perspective.

RESPECTABLE CABO VERDEAN MEN

Honorable, fathers, grandfathers, uncles and cousins where are you? Stand up and take charge in helping the females heal the wounds of the past. Start taking strong positions such as: "I am not going to allow this destructive behavior to continue." Stop the perpetrator from making sexualized comment to minors, stop them from touching minors, and demand they show respect, demand safety for the minors. It is never too late to start protecting our females. Where are the honorable men when these girls are being verbally demoralized and sexually abused? Where are the males to stop the perpetrators? It is time for a paradigm shift. Stand tall and become an ally to minors because without your protection, they do not stand a chance in being safe.

CHILD MOLESTER

The characteristics of molesters are similar across culture and class. The vast majority of offenders do not get caught, and they have no criminal records. Molesters usually try to be very charming and friendly. They tend to show an excessive interest in children, and often seduce children with attention, affection and gifts. They begin by being master seducers of children and build trust, and overtime they become the abusers. These are the kindest, amazing family members that all the kids love, and all of the adults' trust. They are masters of lies and manipulation. These are the family members who take all the kids on rides, buy ice cream, give children rides to school or to the movies. These abusers appear to be parents' answered prayers, to alleviate family stress by stepping in and saving the day by meeting the needs of the family.

The child molester also possesses intense sexual attraction to children and these feelings put children at risk. The feelings manifest as the following:

- Thinking often about children.
- Having recurrent sexual thought or fantasies about children.
- Unsuccessful attempts to stop.
- Looking forward to seeing children.
- Solicits information from children and becoming flirtatious.
- Dreams and daydreaming about children.
- Believes children love you and misinterprets kids' affection for sexual interest.
- Becoming sexually aroused thinking about kids or when in their presence.
- Wanting to touch children.

The myth that child molesters are monsters is inaccurate. The community needs to be educated that the child molesters are the males who are kind and helpful and the most unsuspecting persons. However, the good news is that the community is aware who the perpetrators are and the problem is not identifying them, but rather stop providing them with an avenue to continue. Let us unite and focus on protecting the innocent victims.

CHAPTER 4

CABO VERDEAN VIEWS THROUGH MUSIC

<u>Escape</u>
Music of peace and unity
Rescued my mind to escape
Carried my pain in the lyrics
Embraced my tears in a melody
Song of peace and hope

"I WILL SHOUT FOR JOY AND SING YOUR PRAISES, FOR YOU HAVE RANSOMED ME."

– Psalm 71:23-24

The soul of Cabo Verde is expressed in poetry and music. "It would not be an exaggeration to call Cabo Verdeans some of the most musical people on the planet, and the depth of their creativity given the paucity of their population is astounding. Music pulses through the daily life of Cabo Verdianos like blood, binding communities and uniting distant cousins in a celebration of a unique and bountiful culture. Separation has not weakened Cabo Verdianos culture. If anything, it has given it strength as immigrants use music to reflect their love of their homeland."

Since music is a form of communication in this community, some of the music was analyzed here to look at how incest, power dynamics or differences, and cultural rules are portrayed in music – as a reflection of the values and mores within the Cabo Verdean community. All the music discussed here is well known within the Cabo Verdean community.

"NHA MUDJER E TRABADJADERA"
AMADEU FONTES, RELEASED 2000 (BROCKTON, MA).

This song attacks a wife who has an affair and was discovered. She was presented as a woman who followed cultural roles by being a good cook and hard worker. However, she is then shamed and humiliated by her husband who feels she left all for nothing. Extramarital affairs are something that men do often in the culture. It is seen as a positive and a position of power for men to have more than one woman. It speaks of his status in the community. It takes a man with material wealth to keep more than one woman. However, when a woman does it, she is shamed and crucified with disgust by both males and females in the community.

UN STA DJOBE PADRI KI CASAN"
AMADEU FONTES, RELEASED 1999

This song depicts the differences in roles between women and men. The man is remembering how wonderful Cabo Verde is because women know that their place is behind the man and take on an identity through the man, but how powerless he feels in America where he feels women have more rights and privileges and the support of the police, which leaves men feeling helpless and powerless. The men are also yearning to reclaim their power and control.

"TAM TAM 2000"
RECORDED 1980 (PORTUGAL)

This song talks about a man from one of the islands. It talks about his rage and violence and that women represent a sexual object for him to do with as he pleases. The violence toward women is glorified as the singer talked about himself hitting a woman as he became enraged.

"MARIA GERALDA"
RELEASED 1982 (CABO VERDE)

The musical lyrics describe a woman with a son; the community is questioning his paternity. She replies that her baby has no father, and that her baby is innocent but has no family. This response suggests that the community may know who the father of the child is, but ignores it and puts the responsibility on the female and not on the male. This blame puts the responsibility for moral uprightness all on the women; they primarily bear the burdens for most "sins" within the community. Perhaps this song demonstrates how incest is easily perpetuated because often the female children are blamed for their own exploitation and abuse.

"SUFA"

DANI LOPES, RELEASED 1987 (PORTUGAL)

The lyrics describe power differentiation within the Cabo Verdean culture. The music is about a woman who has intercourse with a man and then asks the man to furnish her house and provide her with material wealth. The song starts with the woman screaming her wishes to this man as they are intimate. She screams, "will you provide me with a house, bed, table, sofa etc.?" This song is a clear picture of the power difference in the culture. It may also be saying that the woman cannot provide these things for herself. She has to sell her body to get a house. The male alone holds the power. This belief is overtly manifested when people can hear a woman screaming and ignore it as long as she is in an intimate relationship with a man and it is unknown if the relation is coerced or not. Female dis-empowerment has become normative. Again, this view has shifted over time where women are more empowered and taking a stand.

"TUNGA, TUNGUINHA"

CESARIA EVORA, RELEASED 1970

This song talks about a female-male interaction. The phrase "I grabbed her breast, I tore her underwear" glorifies what appears to be a rape scene or an interaction that started consensually, but changed to become violent. Cabo Verdean females' actions are for the pleasure and comfort of males implying their bodies are not even their own.

This music symbolizes and even emphasizes the roles/expectations that are placed on the genders. The responsibility appears to lie on the women when societal norms are not followed. This expectation was best stated by a respected elder woman in the community who reported her role as submissive to her husband. She enjoyed taking care of her husband and was friendly to all his mistresses and their children. She believed strongly that:

> Men are like saws, and their job is to cut down trees. The more trees they cut the better. People want to buy a sharp saw that can cut easily and with efficiency. The saw has to be smooth and soft around the edges and flexible in order to cut trees quickly. It also has to be quiet. This is very important because it can catch the tree by surprise and be more successful with trees because it's quiet and the tree may assume it will be gentle and kind. Women are like trees. Their job is to wait to be cut down or get out of the way if they can, which may be very difficult depending on the saw (personal communication, 2001).

This communication depicts the traditional views of an elderly grandmother. This view puts women in a hopeless position. However, our women have always been powerful and strong, and if united with other women, they will have immense power to weaken the saws and even remove them from the garden of hope and peace. Without saws, the flowers will blossom fully.

CHAPTER 5

CABO VERDEAN FAMILY MODELS

Family
Ultimate betrayal, most dreadful violation
My protector, my nurturer and my blood
Hatred, fear, confusion and madness blossoming
Childhood, innocence and happiness aborted
Endurance and faith prevails

"BUT THOSE WHO HOPE IN THE LORD WILL RENEW THEIR STRENGTH. THEY WILL

SOAR ON WINGS LIKE EAGLES; THEY WILL RUN AND NOT GROW WEARY,

THEY WILL WALK AND NOT BE FAINT"

– Isaiah 40:31

Cabo Verdean models of family are based on the concept of communal care in the family structure and the connection within the families. In actual situations, this meant that no one was left to fend for him or herself. One person's pain is shared by the community. The progress of the family or even the wellbeing of all the families is dependent upon uplifting the potential of all to succeed. What affects one, affects the other. When one hurts, the other feels the pain. When one person in the community rejoices, another cries tears of joy. This concept raises the question of whether or not these values apply to women and children, the most vulnerable in such a patriarchally-driven society/culture. The women "sufri caladu" or suffer in silence, and children are meant to be seen and not heard as traditional practices dictate, but this also has shifted with changes over time.

This communal model has many advantages. However, when problems arise like incest, the individual is immersed in pain. Incest can tear apart even the strongest relationship. How can communal notions of care be called upon when the pain is deeply personal and individual? In such times, it is hard to think about sharing pain when the first thought to cross one's mind is, "this is too terrible, and who would ever believe me?" What is the answer? Some turn to God while others try to forget about it and move on while suffering in silence.

INCEST AND FAMILY DYNAMICS

Incest is difficult to accept when the abuser is also part of the family. Family loyalty is divided between the abuser and the victim. This kind of turmoil only adds to the suffering. The victims of incest often become the scapegoat and this tendency helps to keep the family intact. The parents displace their problems onto the daughter and blame her for any conflict that they cannot resolve. They are unable to accept responsibility for the incest (Thornman, 1983).

Thornman (1983) discussed four ways of discounting an incestuous relationship that both parents sometimes use when confronted with evidence of sexual abuse. First, denying that the problem exists; second, discounting the significance of the problem; third, defining the problem as insolvable; and last, blaming the problem on the child.

As the scapegoat, the daughter is placed in a dilemma. If she reveals the incest, she will be held responsible for the disintegration of the family. If she remains silent, she will be accused of encouraging the incest and defined as a "bad" child. Either alternative reinforces her position of scapegoat (Thornman, 1983, p. 12).

Most Cabo Verdean parents and families actually accuse the victim of lying about the abuse. Those families that do believe the victim may encourage or pressure the child not to report it in order to avoid the scandal and deal with the problem within the family.

According to my research, the community may feel that keeping the child away from the offender while in the same home is a sufficient "prevention response." This may also be harmful to the victim.

According to McIntyre (1981), the patriarchal structure (males are with significantly more power and privilege than females) is a cultural barrier for women reporting the abuse. The power in the incestuous family is usually concentrated with the father. He holds the dominant position and intimidates and controls all other family members. This unequal distribution of power paves the way for an incestuous father-daughter relationship to occur. Since the other family members have no power, they will be unable to offer any assistance.

An emerging perspective on the role of mothers in incestuous families is the feminist viewpoint. The proponents of this view defend mothers by linking the sexual abuse of children by their father to the social and cultural values of a patriarchal society. According to McIntyre (1981) and Wattenberg (1985), men are seen as powerful, dominant and as having the right to own women and children. Within the family, children grow up in an oppressive situation where the father is powerful and the mother is powerless. Children learn to comply with their fathers' wishes. McIntyre (1981, p. 465) claims that the ". . . patriarchal cultural dominance sets the stage for incest to occur."

CHANGE CULTURAL BARRIERS

Illiteracy can be a cultural barrier due to the fact most Cabo Verdean traditions are passed on orally and indirectly through storytelling. This storytelling fosters a culture that is immersed in the oral tradition. Generational storytelling subsequently implies veracity to orally transmitted information. In addition, the limited access to formal education and the low percentage of literacy in older generations makes it difficult to educate people who are entrenched in the oral tradition.

Some Cabo Verdean children in America take care of the younger siblings and keep the house clean, and cook while the parents work two to three jobs in order to support the family. These children also learn to speak the English language and become the interpreter for the family.

The role reversal creates tremendous problems for children in America. Generational boundaries are blurred and children are expected to perform beyond their capacities. This reversal is also confusing for the daughter, particularly to her self-identity, as her childhood includes experiences outside of the normal American range. She may never have been allowed to be a child. The Cabo Verdean pattern replicates the most common forms of dysfunction found in American incestuous families, the role reversal between mother and daughter. Daughters assume the responsibilities of the mother; that is, managing the household, supervising the siblings and catering to the needs of the father. The daughter provides the care and nurturance that the family needs and which the mother cannot supply (Thornman, 1983).

SEXUAL ABUSE IN CABO VERDE

According to the human rights report on Cabo Verde:

"Child abuse and mistreatment, sexual violence against children, and juvenile prostitution are continuing problems, exacerbated by chronic poverty, large unplanned families, and traditional high level of immigration of adult men. In July 1998, the newspaper "A Semana" reported several cases of sexual abuse against children and adolescents. The newspaper observed that the violations often occur in the victims' families and often are known by neighbors and relatives who prefer to keep silent. The inefficiencies of the judicial system make it difficult for the mass media and government institutions to address the problem" (1998 Human Rights Report, p. 5).

According to the U.S. State Department's Cabo Verde 2013 Trafficking in Persons Report:

"The Government of Cape Verde demonstrated minimal efforts to combat human trafficking during the year; however, it did not prosecute or convict any trafficking offenders. Cape Verdean law does not specifically prohibit all forms of trafficking, though several existing statutes cover certain forms. Article 14 of the labor code prohibits forced labor and Article 271 of the penal code outlaws slavery, both of which prescribe sufficiently stringent penalties of six to 12 years' imprisonment. Article 148 of the penal code outlaws facilitating prostitution of children under the age of 16 and prescribes sufficiently stringent penalties of two to eight years' imprisonment for victims under 14 years and one to five years for victims aged 14 or 15. These penalties are not commensurate with penalties for other grave crimes, such as rape. The penal code does not prohibit or punish those who facilitate the prostitution of children aged 16 and 17. Investigations into sex crimes involving children aged 14 and 15 require complaints from the child's legal guardian; government officials indicate that no such case has ever been reported to police. Prostituted children aged 14 to 17 are rendered virtually invisible to law enforcement and social welfare officials under existing law, granting impunity to those who profit from their exploitation."

"During the year, the judicial police investigated at least two cases of child prostitution reported by the ICCA. In February 2013, the government began prosecution of three men involved in the prostitution of teenage boys between the ages of 12 and 14 transported from Praia to other parts of the island of Santiago for prearranged clients. The second case involved the prostitution of children on the island of Sal. The government did not provide information regarding the status of these cases. It did not provide any specialized training for officials on the identification or prosecution of trafficking offenses. There were no reports of trafficking-related corruption during the year; corruption is generally not a significant issue in Cape Verde."

I believe that corruption occurs in all forms of government and society and Cabo Verde is not immune to it. It may be more prevalent in underdeveloped nations due to lack of transparency and accountability. Cabo Verde needs to take a stronger stance to improve its identification and provide treatment for victims of sexual abuse. The government may intentionally or unintentionally minimize and dismiss the seriousness of this issue. I challenge the Cabo Verdean government to develop protections for the victims and provide services that are realistic for the people and accountability for the child molesters by implementing and enforcing the laws.

In Addition, because of Catholic influences, Cabo Verdean families have difficulties discussing sexual matters and intimacy openly. Since many of the girls feel socially restricted regarding sexual matters, it seems highly unlikely that they may report or even seek medical treatment, or any kind of treatment or spiritual healing for sexual abuse.

Sometimes, there exists a complete suppression of sexual display. In these families, sex is never mentioned; sex is a particularly difficult subject for the mothers. Will (1983) notes that these families present to the outside world with an ideal image of traditional gender roles. The father maintains a powerful patriarchal image with reciprocal submissiveness by the mother's very rigid views on sexuality.

However, it appears that in some incestuous families, there is a very permissive attitude toward sex. Mothers sometimes contribute to this by encouraging inappropriate sexual contact between father and daughter. The line between normal expressions of affection and sexual abuse becomes blurred, and the parents use the child to fulfil their own needs for sexual stimulation thereby setting the stage for incest to occur (Will, 1983, p. 18).

Most, if not all, Cabo Verdeans would agree that incest is wrong. However, the community does not confront or deal with these problems. They tend to ignore its presence. One may wonder that if the community was able to discuss sex, would there be some likelihood that these traumatic events would be avoided? Will (1983) notes that the homeostatic mechanism working within the incestuous family is extremely powerful as evidenced by the way in which the family often closes ranks and denies the existence of incest after it has been disclosed. Often, the daughter herself may withdraw the accusation of incest or remain silent and uncooperative within the family. This is how Cabo Verdean families handle incest.

A common feature which contributes to the homeostasis is the intense fear that the family will break up. This fear of abandonment is so pervasive that incestuous relationships are tolerated as a means of avoiding family disintegration (Will, 1983 p. 5). This fear is huge for Cabo Verdean survivors of incest due to the strong family bond and its importance in the community. Given the importance of family to the Cabo Verdean community, it makes sense that women and children will do whatever it takes to keep family intact and child molesters depend on this silence to remain untouchable. The next chapters will look at how we can protect our children.

CHAPTER 6
PSYCHOLOGICAL IMPACT OF SEXUAL ABUSE

Shattered Reality
Love introduced nightmares
Hands touched the untouchable
Sadness and death consumes
Fear takes permanent residency
Waiting for healing

"But I will restore you to health and heal your wounds, declares the Lord."

– Jeremiah 30:17

The following list of mental problems was taken from the Diagnostic and Statistical Manual of Mental Disorders (DSM-5). This list is not a complete checklist of symptoms, but a synopsis of impacts. This list will detail the seriousness of how sexual abuse impacts the body, mind and spirit. Only a qualified professional can diagnose a person with the following diagnoses.

POST-TRAUMATIC STRESS DISORDER (PTSD)

• PTSD is a mental health condition that develops following exposure to chronic, long-lasting traumatic events like incest.

• Feeling upset by things that remind you of what happened.

• Having nightmares, vivid memories, or flashbacks of the events that makes you feel like it is happening all over again.

• Feeling emotionally cut off from others.

• Feeling numb or losing interest in things you used to care about.

• Feeling constantly on guard.

• Feeling irritated or having angry outbursts.

- Having difficulty sleeping.

- Having trouble concentrating.

- Being jumpy or easily startled.

- Frequently avoiding places or things that remind you of what happened.

- Consistently drinking or using drugs to numb your feelings.

- Consider harming yourself or others.

- Start working all the time to occupy your mind.

- Traumatic nightmares. Note: children may have frightening dreams without content related to the trauma(s).

- Dissociative reactions (e.g., flashbacks) which may occur on a continuum from brief episodes to complete loss of consciousness. Note: children may reenact the event in play.

- Intense or prolonged distress after exposure to traumatic reminders.

- Marked physiologic reactivity after exposure to trauma-related stimuli.

- Irritable or aggressive behavior.

- Self-destructive or reckless behavior.

- Hypervigilance.

- Exaggerated startle response.

- Problems in concentration.

- Sleep disturbance.

- Depersonalization: experience of being an outside observer of or detached from oneself (e.g., feeling as if "this is not happening to me" or one were in a dream).

- Derealization: experience of unreality, distance, or distortion (e.g., "things are not real").

In a recent study, women who reported childhood sexual abuse were five times more likely to be diagnosed with PTSD compared to nonvictims (Coid et al., 2003).

MAJOR DEPRESSION DISORDER (MDD)

- Feeling sad most of the time.

- Feeling tired or having low energy most of the day.

- Loss of interest in activities once enjoyed.

- Changes in appetite, weight loss or weight gain.

- Trouble concentrating.

- Difficulty sleeping.

- Feeling worthless.

- Feeling helpless or hopeless.

- Feeling anxious or agitated.

- Unexplained headaches, stomach problems or muscular/skeletal pain.

- Thoughts of death or suicide.

In one study, the rate of lifetime depression among childhood rape survivors was 52% compared to 27% among nonvictims (Saunders et al., 1999).

GENERAL ANXIETY DISORDER (GAD)

- An unhealthy tendency to worry about a variety of things (e.g., work, family, money, health).

- A tendency to anticipate the worst and to worry over trivial matters.

- An inability to control your worry.

- Physical symptoms, such as fatigue, headaches, restlessness, muscle tension and trouble sleeping.

- Behavioral symptoms, such as irritability.

BIPOLAR DISORDER

Bipolar disorder, formerly called manic depression, causes extreme mood swings that include emotional highs (mania or hypomania) and lows (depression).

- Bipolar I Disorder. You have had at least one manic episode. The manic episode may be preceded by or followed by hypomanic or major depressive episodes. Mania symptoms cause significant impairment in your life and may require hospitalization or trigger a break from reality (psychosis).

- Bipolar II Disorder. You have had at least one major depressive episode lasting at least two weeks and at least one hypomanic episode lasting at least four days, but you have never had a manic episode. Major depressive episodes or the unpredictable changes in mood and behavior can cause distress or difficulty in areas of your life.

- Cyclothymic Disorder. You have had at least two years – or one year in children and teenagers – of numerous periods of hypomania symptoms (less severe than a hypomanic episode) and periods of depressive symptoms (less severe than a major depressive episode). During that time, symptoms occur at least half the time and never go away for more than two months. Symptoms cause significant distress in important areas of your life.

SOMATIZATION DISORDER

- Disproportionate and persistent thoughts about the seriousness of health complaints (e.g., gastrointestinal pain, physical pain, and sexual dysfunction).

- Persistently high anxiety about health issues.

- Excessive time and energy spent on health concerns.

SEXUAL DYSFUNCTIONS

Sexual dysfunction generally is classified into four categories:

- Desire Disorders. Lack of sexual desire or interest in sex.

- Arousal Disorders. Inability to become physically aroused or excited during sexual activity.

- Orgasm Disorders. Delay or absence of orgasm (climax).

- Pain Disorders. Pain during intercourse.

BORDERLINE PERSONALITY DISORDER (BPD)

- A pattern of intense and unstable relationships with family, friends, and loved ones, often swinging from extreme closeness and love (idealization) to extreme dislike or anger (devaluation).

- Distorted and unstable self-image or sense of self.

- Impulsive and often dangerous behaviors, such as spending sprees, unsafe sex, substance abuse, reckless driving, and binge eating.

- Recurring suicidal behaviors or threats or self-harming behavior, such as cutting.

- Intense and highly changeable moods, with each episode lasting from a few hours to a few days.

- Chronic feelings of emptiness.

- Inappropriate, intense anger or problems controlling anger.

- Having stress-related paranoid thoughts.

- Having severe dissociative symptoms, such as feeling cut off from oneself, observing oneself from outside the body, or losing touch with reality.

OBSESSIVE-COMPULSIVE PERSONALITY DISORDER (OCD)

- Is preoccupied with details, rules, lists, order, organization, or schedules to the extent that the major point of the activity is lost.

- Shows perfectionism that interferes with task completion (e.g., is unable to complete a project because his or her own overly strict standards are not met).

- Is excessively devoted to work and productivity to the exclusion of leisure activities and friendships (not accounted for by obvious economic necessity).

- Is over conscientious, scrupulous, and inflexible about matters of morality, ethics, or values (not accounted for by cultural or religious identification).

- Is unable to discard worn-out or worthless objects even when they have no sentimental value.

- Is reluctant to delegate tasks or to work with others unless they submit to exactly his or her way of doing things.

- Adopts a miserly spending style toward both self and others; money is viewed as something to be hoarded for future catastrophes.

- Shows significant rigidity and stubbornness.

AVOIDANT PERSONALITY DISORDER

- Avoids occupational activities that involve significant interpersonal contact, because of fears of criticism, disapproval, or rejection.

- Is unwilling to get involved with people unless certain of being liked.

- Shows restraint within intimate relationships because of the fear of being shamed or ridiculed.

- Is preoccupied with being criticized or rejected in social situations.

- Is inhibited in new interpersonal situations because of feelings of inadequacy.

- Views themselves as socially inept, personally unappealing, or inferior to others.

- Is unusually reluctant to take personal risks or to engage in any new activities because they may prove embarrassing.

DEPENDENT PERSONALITY DISORDER (DPD)

- Inability to make decisions, even everyday decisions like what to wear without the advice and reassurance of others.

- Avoidance of adult responsibilities by acting passive and helpless; dependence on a spouse or friend to make decisions like where to work and live.

- Intense fear of abandonment and a sense of devastation or helplessness when relationships end; a person with DPD often moves right into another relationship when one ends.

- Oversensitivity to criticism.

- Pessimism and lack of self-confidence, including a belief that they are unable to care for themselves.

- Avoidance of disagreeing with others for fear of losing support or approval.

- Inability to start projects or tasks because of a lack of self-confidence.

- Difficulty being alone.

- Willingness to tolerate mistreatment and abuse from others.

- Placing the needs of their caregivers above their own.

- Tendency to be naive and to fantasize.

NARCISSISTIC PERSONALITY DISORDER

- Having an exaggerated sense of self-importance.

- Expecting to be recognized as superior even without achievements that warrant it.

- Exaggerating your achievements and talents.

- Being preoccupied with fantasies about success, power, brilliance, beauty or the perfect mate.

- Believing that you are superior and can only be understood by or associate with equally special people.

- Requiring constant admiration.

- Having a sense of entitlement.

- Expecting special favors and unquestioning compliance with your expectations.

- Taking advantage of others to get what you want.

- Having an inability or unwillingness to recognize the needs and feelings of others.

- Being envious of others and believing others envy you.

- Behaving in an arrogant or haughty manner.

DRUGS OR ALCOHOL ABUSE

- Failing to fulfill major role obligations (e.g., poor work performance or repeated absences from work or school, neglect of children or household).

- Using substances in situations that are physically hazardous (e.g., driving an automobile or operating machinery when impaired by substance use).

- Experiencing substance-related legal problems (e.g., substance-related disorderly conduct, DUI).

- Continuing to use substances despite having persistent or recurrent social or interpersonal problems caused or worsened by the effects of substances (e.g., arguments or physical fights).

DRUGS AND ALCOHOL DEPENDENCY

- *Tolerance*, which refers to the need to increase amounts of the substance in order to achieve intoxication or the desired effect. A sign of tolerance is a diminished effect with continued use of the same amount of the substance.

- *Withdrawal*, which is the development of a substance-specific syndrome when substance use is stopped or decreased. The type and length of withdrawal symptoms vary depending upon the substance. A sign of withdrawal is the need to take the same or similar substance in order to avoid withdrawal symptoms.

- Taking substances in a larger amount or over a longer period of time.

- Wanting to cut down or control substance use, but may not be able to do so.

- Spending a lot of time and effort doing whatever is necessary to obtain the substance or recovering from the negative effects of using the substance.

- Giving up or reducing social, occupation, or recreational activities because of substance use.

- Continue to use the substance despite awareness of physical or psychological problems that are either caused or worsened by substance use.

Incest is destructive and damaging and there are other psychological affects not covered. It is past time for the community to face this destructive trauma and face the damages and provide a healing and loving environment for the voiceless to speak and be heard.

National Association of Adult Survivors of Child Abuse reports **What Are The Effects Of Child Sexual Abuse?**
The experience of sexual abuse for a child distorts her or his self-concept, orientation to the world and affective capabilities.
High rates of depression, anxiety, substance abuse, dissociative disorders, interpersonal dysfunction, sexual problems and suicidal ideation have all been identified to varying degrees among men and women who survive child sexual abuse.
Child sexual assault victims are 4.7 times more likely to be the subsequent victim of a sex crime.
Adolescents with a history of sexual abuse are significantly more likely to engage in sexual behavior that puts them at risk for HIV infection.
A 1996 report from the U.S. Department of Justice estimated rape and sexual abuse of children to cost $1.5 billion in medical expenses and $23 billion total annually to U.S. victims.
When sexually abused children are not treated, society must later deal with resulting problems such as mental health issues, drug and alcohol abuse, crime, suicide and the perpetuation of a cycle of sexual abuse.

CHAPTER 7

DAMAGES TO THE CHILDREN

Took the Blame
Mind that witnessed the hell,
Body survived the assault
Gentle hands that kill
Destroyer without remorse
Violated our secret places
Endured the pain and the shame,
In the end took the blame
Escaped into fantasy.

"CHILDREN ARE A GIFT FROM THE LORD. THEY ARE A REWARD FROM HIM."
– Psalm 127:3

According to Tavris (1992), in an ideal family or an ideal culture, children learn to respect their bodies, to find the beauty of their uniqueness, and to discover the names of all their body parts with equal delight. They know when to be proud and when to be private. They respect the variety within their own gender and differences from each other without criticism. Children whose early lives are free of abuse learn from adults that they own their bodies; they can decide who touches them and how. When they must rely on others to take care of their needs, they learn that there is safety in being taken care of, that touches feel warm and reassuring, and that when something goes wrong with their bodies, it can and should be helped or corrected. They learn that their bodies deserve respect, positive regard, and proper attention. They learn what appropriate touch is and what is not (Tavris, p. 30).

However, this expectation is often not the case for sexually abused children. Among Cabo Verdean children, some are never taught about their bodies or sexuality. Families believe this topic to be taboo and have difficulty addressing questions that sons and daughters may ask. Sex education is not acceptable to most of the parents.

Incest is a problem that exists in every culture. In America, there are laws to protect minors and treatment for them. There are consequences for perpetrators. Since our community does not confront or deal with these problems, it has gotten out of control due to a lack of accountability and consequences. I will take a guess that the prevalence is triple, if not more, in a community where there is no fear of consequences. It is a problem when a society becomes complacent and ignores the light of happiness and innocence disappearing from its children's eyes.

The strength of Cabo Verdean families is the presence of extended family members. While this strength is notable, it will also create opportunities for increased incest and sexual abuse. When abuse occurs, these extended family connections may serve as a barrier for Cabo Verdean kids to avoid the perpetrators. When a child is sexually abused by a family member, this beautiful girl learns that her body is dirty because it is touched at night or in secret and shame is introduced. This pure child is no longer innocent because her protector has shown her things only adults should know. Her question goes unanswered because the person who should make her feel special about her body has destroyed it. The person who should teach her pride and self-respect has shamed her and disrespected her body in the worst way. She begins to hate her body and what it represents.

Incest leaves both visible and invisible marks and it invades every part of one's life. It is very important to be aware of how it is manifesting in your daily life. The lasting effects of incest are listed below but are not limited to the list. Individuals may develop different symptoms from one another depending on the age when the abuse began, how long it lasted and who the perpetrators were. These factors play a huge part on how impacted one will be. This trauma to the body and soul will shape how we cope, relate, trust and live authentically.

HOW SEXUAL ABUSE IMPACTS CHILDREN
PSYCHOLOGICAL SIGNS

The signs that children are being sexually abused are often present, but parents need to pay attention to them. If the parent is a survivor of incest and has not worked through her issues, she may not be able to see the signs in her own child.

Some warning signs that should be further discussed to verify if sexual abuse is occurring: your child begins waking up during the night sweating, screaming or shaking with nightmares; complaining of pain while urinating or having a bowel movement; exhibiting symptoms of genital infections such as offensive odors; wetting the bed; showing unusual fear of a certain place or location and loss of appetite; complaining of stomachaches and headaches; complaining of difficulty in walking or sitting; experiencing pain or itching in the genital area; regressing to behaviors too young for them; communicating a sudden reluctance to be alone with a family member; and losing interest in previously enjoyable activities.

CULTURAL EXAMPLES

The common ways our culture deals with these signs is to minimize the child's complaints and blame the child for the torn or stained clothing, while paying no attention to the child's complaints of pain while being bathed. Parents often do not recognize the signs and may not know how to make inquiries.

Some kids regress to thumb-sucking and bed-wetting or have academic problems. Some may exhibit seductive behaviors and obsessively rub their genitals on others, trying to do to others what is being done to them. Some children display sexual knowledge beyond what is normal for their age for instance making orgasmic sounds during masturbation. Others have an extreme fear of being touched or fears of going to bed. Some become secretive or unusually aggressive. Again, these behaviors go unnoticed or the child gets reprimanded for the change. For instance, a child may be told, "Do not be rude to your uncle, sit on his lap and apologize for being rude." "Why are you scared of grandpa? He is very nice to you and he is the reason we are all in America. Go give him a hug and apologize. I do not know where she is picking up this behavior, maybe from school." Or the child may get physical punishment.

NOTE TO PARENTS

Parents, your children are the precious gifts God has entrusted you to raise, protect and love. I know it is hard. It is unbearable to accept the idea that the danger to your child is sleeping in the next room or in your bed. Moms, we have to pray for the courage and strength to stand and protect the innocent child. Let us shift the focus from working overtime and having the best house with the best furniture to having a child who has a happy childhood by not allowing family members to molest or have sex with them. The kids do not need the best clothing; they need a mother and father who protects them by keeping them safe and innocent and not allowing others to rob them of a childhood.

DAMAGES TO ADOLESCENTS

Hell
To stop your loving hands
Silent tears and silent screams
You did not see or hear
Pain, scars, pleading eyes
Wired fences and land mines
Intrusion continued
Too tired, closed my eyes
Left my body
And surrendered
To the loving hands
Birth in hell

"GOD IS OUR REFUGE AND STRENGTH, AN EVER-PRESENT HELP IN TROUBLE."
– Psalm 46:1

According to O'Brien (1998), the most seriously compromised task among victims was the establishment of a positive sense of self. The victims tended to see themselves as "damaged goods" and were afraid that potential suitors would reject them. Adolescents feels that there must have been something within them wrong to begin with since the perpetrator had chosen them and their mothers had not protected them. This feeling is often compounded when social service agencies remove the abused child from the home (in such cases where abuse has occurred in home). Reality testing and body image are also compromised. The incest relationship damages the victim's sense of self as her perception and feelings are ignored or denied (O'Brien, 1998, p. 6).

Teenage years are a time of growth, development, exploration, identity formation and fun. Instead, a victim of incest is forced to focus on surviving sexual advances of an adult family member. She is trying to survive the land mine. Therefore, she does not make the same developmental progress as an adolescent who received unconditional love, support, and guidance. It is during adolescence that the real consequences of being sexually abused occur. This crucial time of puberty and sexual energy can be a scary time for teens that were or are still being sexually abused.

As the child enters puberty, it is a natural time of confusion and needing guidance. She is again failed as the perpetrator continues to seek sexual pleasure from his own blood and ignores his responsibility to guide, protect and help. She continues to be alone, lost, confused, terrified and stays praying no one finds out. She holds all the blame and physically tries to hide the pain by overeating, drinking, using drugs, dressing in layers or too provocatively, constantly second guessing her decisions, not trusting her instincts, not saying what is truly felt but hiding it in sarcasm, jokes, or staying silent. This beautiful and pure teen lives in constant fear and darkness because she has taken all the blame and continues to have a relationship with the perpetrators for the family and for the culture and for her survival. She becomes the sacrificed one.

Teens that are not sexually abused are focusing on their looks and enjoying their sexual development and the development of their body with pride, joy, fears, frustration and enjoying sexual attention from their peers. Meanwhile, the sexually abused teen is terrified and fearful of the changes and filled with disgust for her body while trying to hide the changes in their body. At this time, the perpetrators become more interested and sexual encounters may increase. Often, when these girls try to stop the abuse, they are told by the perpetrators, "You know it is because of what I have been doing to you that your breasts are developing. They are mine and very beautiful. What we are doing is ok, we are family. I will teach you how to be a lady so that you will be experienced when you have a boyfriend. How dare you stop me? I have done my best not to hurt you when are you sad. This is love, no one will believe you. I will kill you if you tell, I will kill myself if you tell or walk away from me. I will kill your parents, no one will believe you, it's your fault." A statement like this destroys any joy a teen might have in her development and instead takes permanent residency in darkness and shame. How does one survive adolescence?

PSYCHOLOGICAL SIGNS

An abused adolescent girl or boy feels helpless, dirty, confused, and power-less and has severe internal pain leading to self-blame and self-hatred. Negative self-images come into play: "I am bad, no one loves me, no one could love me, I am unlovable, and dirty. It's my fault, I am horrible. I wish I was dead, I do not want my body to change, please do not look at me." Adolescence is a time of dating and taking pride in one's appearance and welcoming the changes in one's body. However, most feel shame and disgust and are terrified by the changes.

One has to learn the most debilitating lesson, that people who love us also hurt us. The expression of caring is presumed to be followed by harm or danger, which is not a great setup for developing trusting and loving relationships. In order to deal with the anxiety and fear of forming relationships and facing our body, we develop coping strategies called somatic complaints, which includes migraines, sexual pain, menstrual pain, intestinal complaints, stomach ache, nausea, head-ache, back pain, and painful shoulders; in short, all kinds of chronic pain may occur. The pain is often unexplainable and it continues into adulthood.

Some girls become sexually promiscuous having poor boundaries. Promiscuity becomes a form of gaining control over what was taken. Some may become sexually provocative, dressing and talking in a manner that puts them at risk of further sexual exploitation. Others merge sexual behavior and aggression and become the victimizers of other children. How do parents handle these behaviors in their children? It is handled with insults and verbal abuse, instead of realizing that these were the same girls we failed to protect.

Others avoid all form of sexual contact and become submissive, passive, helpless, avoid conflict, become perfectionistic, and want to please others, feeling detached and emotionally numb. They often have headaches or stomach pains. Those of us presenting this way to cope are ignored by the community and are left alone to internalize self-hate. The comments family often makes are, "You are pretty, why don't you dress nicer? Stop wearing loose clothing, you have a nice body. Go out with your friends. You are strange. Why don't you be more like her? How do you expect to find a husband looking like that? You are not going out with me looking like that."

CULTURAL EXAMPLES

I always thought it was comical that my parents were very clear in their rules that I was not to go on school fieldtrips, have no male friends over or go out with them, and not to go on outings, unless with family as a form of protection. However, they never acknowledged that the danger was not in going on school trips or from my male friends. The danger was nighttime in my bedroom or doing laundry in the basement. The danger was their 60-year-old+ friends and family they welcomed in their home or in some cases the parents themselves.

I knew a teenager who ran away from home to avoid more sexual abuse and rape by her brother. To survive, she began working at a topless dance club and the community began to blame her, making statements like, "How can she shame her family in that way? How can she be this way? It is clear that she lied about the abuse to leave home and be free. She comes from a respectful family see what she is doing to her life. So much potential and she threw it way. Her parent struggled and came to this country for a better life for her and this is how she thanks them. She is disgraceful. Do not talk to her if you see her, she is bad news." The family shifted the reality of a hopeless victim to blame maybe to eliminate their quilt for overlooking and abandoning her in a time of need.

How quickly the community forgot her anguish and suffering while her parents hugged her rapist and provided him with shelter and love and left her in the cold and alone. Shame on the perpetrator, for robbing and destroying her childhood without considering the destruction and pain it would cause. Shame on the parents for allowing such violation and neglecting to protect and show understanding and compassion when it was most needed. Shame on the community members for not opening their doors to her. Shame on all of us for not hugging her and protecting her. Shame on all of us for allowing another beautiful flower bud to be crushed and shattered and thrown away. This beautiful girl, full of life and potential that we did not protect, yet we are very quick to judge while forgetting our parts in her tragedy.

Another impact of sexual abuse is that it often forces a girl to run away from home ill-equipped to survive in the streets. She is victimized again and is forced to become a teen prostitute forced into sexual trafficking, which has become a serious problem in U.S. The average age is 13 and it is decreasing at an alarming rate. In addition to these girls feeling unsafe at home, they are being pushed to the streets where they are being used as sex slaves. They face multiple daily sexual assaults with no place to return to, being controlled by pimps and drugged against their will to face their hourly duties. I beg us to create safe homes for our girls because the alternative is unimaginable.

PERSONAL EXAMPLES

For me, the teen years were the most difficult time. I was severely depressed and in constant emotional pain, which I masked with a smile, telling jokes and developing an intimate relationship with food. Food became my security blanket, my grounding, and my calming and accepting indulgence. I became very passive and obedient, which expressed my depression. I felt dirty, unwanted and was very fearful of dating and having to tell a boy my shame. I remained fearful they would see it in me somehow or see me as damaged goods. I was very humorous and used sexual jokes and food to cover up my turmoil. In addition, I had friends and had fun. My life was not completely mired in depression, but nighttime was when tears would take over.

NOTE TO TEENAGERS

Teens, I understand the running away, the deliberate disobedience, the abusing drugs and alcohol, the stealing, the skipping school, the using sex to feel better or to get back at parents, the lying, the gambling, the vandalizing, the cheating, the abusing siblings, friends, peers, or boyfriends/girlfriends, the taking dangerous risks, the joining gangs, tattoos, piercing, prostitution, the forcing of sexual acts on other children, the cutting to release pain and the attempting suicide, the addictive behavior and the silent pain. However, these behaviors are not helping you heal, they are worsening your pain and worsening your suffering. You are worthy. You are deserving of a better life.

We need to say to all the teens we are sorry we failed you. We are sorry for all the pain you endured alone. We are sorry no one helped. We are sorry no one is seeing your pain today. We are sorry your innocence was destroyed and your beautiful body was violated. We are so very sorry those meant to love and protect you did the most harm. Today, you can claim your right to happiness from the shackles of your past. This freedom can be claimed with talking to a trusted adult, a therapist, prayers and allowing God to renew you and remove the sting of the past. You are wonderfully made in his image.

DAMAGES TO ADULTHOOD

Alone I stand
The constant sorrow and pain I hide.
Childhood shattered to pieces
So many families witnessed yet no one saw
I stand in the garden of my childhood wondering was that me
For that girl is no more. He took it all
Can you see the ocean in my eyes?
Alone I stand in this gentle fire
Protect me I cried, but alone I stood
An adult child.

"BUT HE SAID TO ME, MY GRACE IS SUFFICIENT FOR YOU,
FOR MY POWER IS MADE PERFECT IN WEAKNESS."
– 2 Corinthians 12:9

PSYCHOLOGICAL IMPACT

As an adult, the sexually abused survivor continues with all the negative feelings from childhood and adolescence and it worsens and intensifies in adulthood, if left untreated. As adults, one is expected to be strong, have a good sense of self and to know what they want. However, trauma leaves scars. Incest creates adults who have become expert in self-sacrificing and self-hate, pretending, presenting a front while living in a shell of confusion and desperation. The Cabo Verdean woman presents well and does an amazing job masking her pain and becoming a resilient survivor, but who is silently killing parts of herself daily with a smile.

The adult survivor suffers from feeling like "damaged goods," often experiences low self-esteem and severe depression, self-mutilation guilt, shame, self-blame, and she continues to crave love, attention and acceptance from the family. She has difficulty trusting others and maintaining relationships. Some have strong feelings of terror, grief, and anger. They avoid both intimacy and emotional bonding and some may shut off all sexual feelings and retreat from all sexual contact due to fears that no one will validate them. Some may experience feelings of hopelessness and desire sexual intimacy, yet have difficulty trusting for the memory it brings. Some have fears of losing control in relationships and feel powerless, some have poor boundaries, some have anxiety, fear, and a tendency towards re-victimization, panic attacks, feel angry with themselves for not being able to stop the abuse, feel angry with the abuser or feel angry with parents or caregivers for not protecting them. Some use food, sex, alcohol and/or drugs to deaden feelings and expel reality temporarily.

CULTURAL COPING EXAMPLES

Denial is the refusal to accept reality or fact, acting as if a painful event, thought or feeling did not exist. Denial is the most commonly used coping strategy in the Cabo Verdean community. Some women, in order to survive and appear functional, deny the abuse to the extent that they no longer believe anything happened. They then develop somatic complaints and have all kinds of chronic pain and this is often how women in our community display any form of mental pain. It is easier to take Tylenol for headaches than to consider alternatives. In order to stay connected to the family, the victim continues to see only the positive attribution of the perpetrator and ignores the bad and eventually will only see the good.

Slanderous conversations are another form of denial or avoidance. One gossips because it is not seen as harmful and it is often done in fun or disguised as information sharing or gathering. The definition of gossip is to spread rumors or secrets, speak about someone maliciously behind their back or repeat something about someone else that you have no right to repeat. Gossip is the destroyer, a character assassination, and it is destructive to Cabo Verdean community. This coping allows one to avoid facing or changing their circumstances and gives them distance from their issues and allows them to focus on others. Often, one uses gossip to pass time and disguise it with concerns, but it is damaging to all involved. Often, one will say, "Have you heard what happened to this person? I knew she was like that, she left her husband, she was no good, she is an awful woman, but has a wonderful husband, her kids will all end up in jail, her kids will never go to college, and she thinks she is better than us." Most women focus on other people so as to avoid looking in their own heart because it is too painful. However, this focus is not healing anyone. Rather, it is creating destruction and is preventing the community from taking care of its wounds and blocks development of genuine trust, healing and growth.

Denial continues as Cabo Verdeans focus on external, superficial things to mask and calm the pain within. The mentality is exemplified in this kind of thinking: "I need a new kitchen, I need to fix the garage, I need a new job, this house is not clean, the house needs to be painted again this year, I am building a 10-bedroom house in Cabo Verde, upgrading furniture unnecessarily, getting a new car because another has one, etc." The focus of the community on materialism serves as a healing block by allowing the focus to shift from pain or insecurities that need attention, to other things less important.

Cabo Verdeans often make the statement "you have changed" with a negative connotation, as if change is not part of life and necessary for growth. The community is terrified of change, growth and separation, but does not apply the same fear and unacceptance to focus on addressing sexual abuse. The culture needs to embrace change and growth in its people and recognize the positive in it and encourage those who wished to improve their knowledge base without put downs or envy. The community tends to be harsh to those who do not hold the same ideals, yet for a population to grow and change, it is integral that all ideas and positions ought to be respected and honored free of judgment, sarcasm and denigration. The community needs to resist making statements like, "Why are you behaving like you did not come from poverty? They used to be nobody... Don't change, remember who you are, you might be educated now, but in Cabo Verde your family was my servants... Don't be superior; I know where your family came from." These statements are based on ignorance and fear of change. People of humble beginnings can achieve greatness the same as those from higher classes. If we are going to change and provide a safer world for our people, it starts by facing our fears and making a radical change in our thinking.

It would be great if we could hold each other accountable and decide to help each other to face and sit with our discomfort and pain. The community is too busy denying and avoiding serious issues that need to be addressed; if the community is to grow into a place of health, balance and peace, there are many changes that need to occur immediately. You may be familiar with the saying, "Before you speak, ask yourself three questions: Is it the truth? Is it kind? Is it necessary?" If we begin to ask ourselves these questions, I imagine we would be listening a lot more and being silent to ponder our role in situations that create safety for someone to share their pain, trusting it will not become the gossip of the day. Let us stop associating or encouraging gossiping from those family members who are known to gossip. When someone starts to gossip, change the subject. Let us begin to be supportive and encourage each other. Let us remove the fake facade and be real with each other without thinking about what people will say or think. Free yourself of worries about what others may say or think and focus on what you think and want because you have no control over others. Put your energy on the one we can change – ourselves. This saying may be the beginning of self-focus and healing. Before responding or criticizing another, stop and start making this statement instead: "God bless them and change me."

Another cultural coping strategy is to be passive because it is familiar, and we can accept familiar misery rather than risk the unknown. Assertion is a difficult concept for most of us and some who appear assertive and confrontational when it comes to standing up for themselves become powerless and are more comfortable suffering than causing another to suffer. We are used to pain, but cannot bear to be the cause of another's suffering. That is why we deny, minimize and move forward. Comments family often use are, "You will never be anything; you will end up in the streets; you don't appreciate your family, we love you but you pushed us away; he would never do something like that, you misunderstood; he was not aware that he was touching your breast, there is no harm; he is a good man, get over it, you liked it, you wanted it; why did you not tell anyone, you make your bed and you lay on it." Often, you may see them roll their eyes when you speak and the hope of being accepted keeps us in a continuous cycle of sexual to emotional abuse and back. We overlook and ignore offences in hopes of keeping the positive image. Families need to pay attention to their words because they are their most dangerous weapon, and people often speak without thinking, which causes irreparable damage. Let us begin to use our words to heal, love and support each other. Maybe we need to focus less on others and more on the masterpiece God created in us. The heart of the righteous ponders how to answer, but the mouth of the wicked pours out evil things, Proverbs 15:28. A gentle tongue is a tree of life, but perverseness in it breaks the spirit, Proverbs 15:4. Know this, my beloved brothers: let every person be quick to hear, slow to speak, slow to anger, James 1:19. With patience a ruler may be persuaded, and a soft tongue will break a bone, Proverbs 25:15.

PERSONAL EXAMPLE

I began psychotherapy when I was 25 years old, shortly after moving to CA. I was blessed to have an amazing therapist who has been so influential in my healing and who I have trusted completely for the past 20 years. As a victim, I believed I deserved to be abused and be the doormat for my family and friends. I believed I did not deserve a good mate, I believed I would never enjoy lovemaking. I believed I could not defend myself because I did not have a right to. I believed my body was not mine to decide. However, with healing, I reclaimed my voice and believe I have a right to say no, to control who enters my personal space, and to defend myself. I healed and was washed anew, and I am blessed that my past has shaped and strengthened the woman I am today.

When I was 25 years old, the flashbacks were too intense and long so I decided it was time to end my life. I reached a point that only suicide was the answer and God intervened by sending a friend to visit me at the exact moment I was going to kill myself. I am so glad I did not kill myself because what was beyond the pain that I could not see was happiness and healing. If I had killed myself, I would not have been able to enjoy this beautiful life I have today. You have to realize it does not matter how bad the storm gets, the sun will always rise in the morning. I never imagined I would get to a place where I felt clean, pure; deserving of the best life has to offer.

I became a survivor who overcame and I continue to work hard to stay on this path. It took many years to get here and you can too. It takes courage to accept what was, what we can never get back, what was lost, mourn the loss, grieve the pain, see the molester as possessing both good and bad qualities, change some relationships, see our values and worth, and reclaim your voice and power. Then, move into a place of healing, of peace, of healthy relationships, of appropriate boundaries, of genuine laughter. Move forward without forgetting the past, and do whatever it takes to secure the safety of future children.

The community needs to begin a healing process of removing the destruction and negativity within the community and foster, support, understanding, praises and love. It is time to change for the better.

NOTE TO ADULTS

Guilt and shame are emotions birthed in sexual abuse survivors. In other words, a person who feels shameful may think that he or she is to blame for the immoral act and is therefore a bad person. My beautiful survivors, this day is where you begin to deconstruct this feeling of shame and guilt because you did nothing wrong. You were violated by your protector. The shame and guilt belong on their doorstep, not in your soul. My dearest sisters and brothers, we also need to accept the fact that the family will not come to save you, to rescue you or to believe you. Locate and develop support systems that will validate and believe you. I am sorry no one is coming to save you. The good news is that as an adult, you can save yourself. I plead that you become yourselves' best friend and protector. Stand tall and free, and reclaim your voice and demand respect for your body from your community because your body, mind and soul are crying out for it. Give yourself the love, acceptance and validation you crave.

CHAPTER 8
PARENTAL RESPONSIBILITY

Healing
House of lies destroyed
Rebuild home of hope and love
Thunder has ceased
Secrets carried by the wind
The sea is calm and peaceful
I spread my wings and soar higher and higher
over the blossoming garden

"WEEPING MAY ENDURE FOR A NIGHT, BUT JOY COMES IN THE MORNING."
– Psalms 30:5

Butman (1983) wrote about sexual abuse in Christian homes. He stated that child sexual abuse may be unreported in religious homes because many fathers may fear losing social status. This fear plays a part in reporting or the lack of it in the Cabo Verdean community.

Terza Lima-Neves (2015) highlights that Cabo Verdean women are active agents of change and can lead in community cohesion including three aspects. First, modern diaspora community building in the U.S. Second, collective identity and the complexities of identity. Lastly, women and community organization. She documented that the first known Cabo Verdean association was founded in New Bedford, MA in 1916. Our Lady of Assumption in New Bedford was established in 1905 as the first Cabo Verdean Catholic church in the U.S. More associations were created as the need arose with an increase in immigration. She reports that most associations were non-political, but a few were. In the 1970's, Cabo Verdeans began building coalitions with African Americans and other immigrant communities and were elected into offices.

Our culture is rich in the celebration of family and connectedness, but it also needs a stronger focus on the children, specifically on recognizing and preventing them from being sexually abused. When a mother allows or overlooks the silent cries of kids and teens being sexually abused. When a girl or boy's innocence is robbed by the adult family members and for generations the community does nothing to protect the children. When the maternal figure conceals it and protects the status of the male and blames the child. With all this cover up and denial, where is the victim? Who is protecting her or him? Who is wiping their tears? Who is easing their fears? Who is holding them? Who is providing hope and security? They are abandoned and made to feel worthless, but the community sees it as a form of protection.

Let us turn our love to the forgotten, the abused, the traumatized, the raped, and the violated. Let us start to validate and apologize, let us start to protect the children. We have the capacity, we have the ability, we have the power. It is past time for the people to experience an earthquake that tears apart the secrecy and gives birth to a home that values children and will protect them and nurture their innocence and protect their right to be children.

DON'T TRUST THE CHILD MOLESTERS ANYMORE

A woman came home and found a frozen snake at her doorstep. She felt sad so she took the snake inside and set it by the fire. She took care of it and within days the snake was doing better. She came home and pets the snake and it bit her. She was shocked, "How can you bite me? I cared you back to life." The snake responded, "What do you expect? I am a snake." Similarly, the community cannot expect a child molester to be with children and act respectfully. It is the community's job to recognize the snakes and keep them out of their homes where they will not bite any children.

The community has been behaving like the woman in the story who felt safe petting a snake with the illusion it would not bite. How can you expect your father not to molest your daughter if he molested you? This mistake that mothers make is common because since they had to deny their own abuse, they no longer view the molesters as abusive thus trusting them to supervise their children. You hope for the best and pray that it will not happen. Since we need to see the best in others, we actually believe our children will be safe with the molesters because part of us still loves them and wants to have a good relationship with them. This belief is why the child molester will molest the daughter, granddaughter and great-granddaughter. It is time to see the snake for what it truly is and not be fooled anymore.

PROTECT THE SURVIVORS

These girls and boys deserve a new environment. It is time they be seen as beautiful, courageous, strong, powerful and lovable. We have the power to change their reality and transform their pain into resiliency and change their status from victim to survivors. All mothers of all ages or those females in the role of mothers need to have a conversation with their daughters. Even if you believe nothing happened to your child, still have the conversation. The process can begin with every mother beginning to talk with their daughter about incest. "I want us to go to lunch and talk. I want to apologize for not protecting you. I am now ready to hear about your pain and suffering. I am ready to hear your secrets. I want to know about the sexual abuse." Give your daughter the love she needs and allow her to also be angry with you. You have to allow her to be angry as this will foster change. Continue to be loving and kind even if she rejects the love. Continue to say, "I am sorry and I am here for whatever you need." Even if she rejects your attempt, continue until she is ready.

- I am sorry.
- I am here for you.
- He will never come to your home.
- What do you want to do, I will support you.
- We are as sick as our secrets, please tell me everything.

Parents, this is going to be difficult, but it needs to be said and understood. **YOU CANNOT SUPPORT YOUR CHILD WHILE YOU MAINTAIN A RELATIONSHIP WITH THE PERSON WHO MOLESTED HIM/HER AND PROBABLY DID THE SAME TO YOU.** We have to face the perpetrators and let them know they are no longer welcome in our home because our priority is to keep our kids safe. No child should ever lose the love and protection of her family while the perpetrator remains sheltered and loved. It would be a wonderful world where the perpetrators get to lose it all for their actions while the victim is surrounded by love.

I am aware of how difficult it is to choose between two family members while both are loved and that choosing destroys the family. You are not removing the perpetrator; he did it himself by exploiting, traumatizing, and destroying, instead of protecting. The pattern is to maintain family unity by sacrificing the child to stay quiet. As easy as this is, it is not the solution because the family is only intact superficially, and you have lost your child by choosing the molester. She may not leave you then, but eventually she will leave and she may never tell you, but will harbor a hidden resentment and even hatred for you for knowingly putting her in a dangerous situation.

MINIMIZING THE PROBLEMS DOES NOT HELP THE VICTIM

Parents deny incest and leave the child alone to face the child molester and in turn eventually deny its existence. Like previous victims, the mother puts her own child in the same situations she was in. Let us be clear that denying does not stop it. Denying does not decrease its effect and definitely does not help the child who is forced to face this evil. Comments often made are "You must have misunderstood. He would not do that; he is respectful, kind and helpful. He loves you how could you say such a thing? Stop provoking the situation. He is a respectful man. He goes to church on Sundays and is very helpful to those in need."

Many times, family members' state, "It is no big deal you just put it behind you and move on. Don't think about it. This is what men do, let it go. You will one day make your own family and this will be behind you. Nothing happened, nothing happened." This denial again does not help the child; rather, it leaves her alone and ashamed, and continues to empower the molester.

Often, when a family tries to support the victim it takes the form of statements like "There is nothing that can be done. Stay out of his way. Don't wear provocative clothing and don't be alone with him, why did you let it happen? You must have liked it." This response is blaming the victim! It does not help the victim; it makes her feel helpless and hopeless. The child's reality is strengthened in that she has no one to help her understand what is happening, or help stop it. Therefore, she submits to the idea that this is her reality to endure. The adult parent who should be helping becomes helpless in front of the child, giving the message that this issue is too much for the adult parents to handle. The child/victim must face it alone. Now, she is in the situation of taking care of the parents. She may internalize her feelings and say, "It did not happen. It has not happened since that one time. I went to him, but I will stop." The mother needs to believe this for her own survival. The child pretends there are no problems, the mother pretends there is no problem, the family unit remains intact and everyone is content except the child who has to continue enduring being molested with no one to save her.

BLAMING THE VICTIMS IS NOT HELPFUL

Some parents and families actually accuse the victim of lying about the abuse or bribe them to lie once the truth is in the open. Those families that believe the victim may cry and pressure the child to keep the secret in order to avoid the scandal and deal with the problem within the family. They may feel that keeping the child away from the offender while living in the same home is a sufficient prevention response. Comments often made are, "You must have wanted it. Why did you not stop it? Why did you allow it to continue for so long?"

When incest is disclosed, some families will actually encourage more contact with the perpetrator to show that there are no negative feelings. Kids are supposed to be seen but not heard. Obeying adults is very important, which creates a barrier in disclosing abuse. The family members spend most of their time together so that, even if one wants to avoid another, it is impossible without creating tension in the family. For example, a mother forced her daughter to greet the man who raped her so the mother could feel good and the community will not talk about her or her daughter's bad manners. Meanwhile, the incident is overlooked allowing more rape to continue. The adult continues to present as hopeless and may even threaten suicide if the secret gets out. Again, the child is enduring the insult to their body and worrying about her parents. Parents, this situation is so unacceptable. What an awful position to place a child or teen in. What a dangerous and scary life for the child to face with the adults refusing to see her or this terrifying position. Let us be the adults and remove this burden from the children.

The whole family needs to be involved in finding different and more helpful ways to communicate. Your words to your child need to be of encouragement, support and love. Some families make statements like, "You must have liked it. I cannot believe you. Why did you not tell me sooner? You provoked the molester." These blaming and ultimately damaging statements need to never come out of our lips as we are helping a victim. The child will be feeling guilty enough as it is, so do not make them feel worse by shaming them or punishing them. Use words of love and kindness like, "I am sorry, you are brave, you are beautiful, you are not to blame, I love you, I will help you through this." Children need to be protected, not violated. They need love and protection, not fear and torture. God is weeping for the community to stand up and begin healing, begin understanding, begin protecting and no longer tolerating the abuse of the innocent.

IT'S EVERYONE'S RESONSIBILITY TO PROTECT THE VICTIM

Men and women need to live in harmony together, and in order for our community to heal the issues need to be addressed and dealt with. We start by beginning to identify the sexual offenders in our community who are, thus far, being protected and sheltered from harm. We go to church on Sundays, praise God and hear messages about God's love and for us to imitate and protect those in need, and yet, we come home and ignore the man molesting our daughters. Women, we need to claim our voices and claim our right to happiness, dignity and respect, and save the next generation.

Mothers have a huge responsibility to all children, and their safety and happiness ought to be top priority. Begin a new tradition of support. Mothers need to start having conversations with their daughters to decide together how changes and interactions will look in their home and together begin the generational healing. Mothers, own your part in perpetuating the abuse and start to create a new vocabulary and expression of love and support for your children. Mothers need each other for unity and to support each other to fight for their kids' safety.

PROTECTION

It is a parent's responsibility to create a safe environment for their children. Create an environment where a child can feel secure to grow and develop into a functioning adult. Safety is a foreign, unknown concept for victims of sexual abuse or incest. It is a human right that was never available. The suggestions to protect a child in this chapter are provided with a communal framework in mind. Options that apply to individualized cultures are not covered as they may be difficult for a collectivistic culture to implement. There are multiple ways to provide safety, but the ones provided in this chapter will be for a culture which values communal over individual values.

KEEPING NON-ABUSED CHILDREN SAFE
CREATE A SAFE ENVIRONMENT

In order to protect the children from being sexually abused, we need to create safety. That means parents need to create an environment where the molesters are not welcomed. The parent will need to have a conversation with the child molester in their family and say, "I care for you and do not want to start problems, but I am going to have a baby and you need to know you will not be welcomed in my home anymore. You need to come up with excuses when there is a function at my home because under no circumstances are you to step in my home or acknowledge my child. What you did will not be repeated with my child." This statement done in private may not change the unity of the family too much and you have given the abuser the burden of coming up with excuses for not going to your home or approaching your child at family functions. You do not have to worry about what will happen because he has to come up with excuses for not visiting your home. The burden of responsibility is on him.

DEVELOP AN OPEN COMMUNICATION

The second point is developing the vocabulary to have conversations with your children to help them own their body, develop appropriate boundaries, and learn to say no. Teaching them about the beauty of their body and when and who can touch them, and for what reason is necessary. Example: "only mama and papa can touch your privates to clean or wash you. Any other reason for touching, you scream, 'No, do not touch me.' You can tell me anything. If someone tells you not to tell mommy, that is when you run and tell me. If they threaten to hurt me, you or any family if you tell, they are lying. That is when you tell me what does not feel right. Has anyone touched you or showed you things that made you feel uncomfortable? Who do you not feel safe with? Mommy's job is to keep you safe, and in order for me to do that, you have to tell me what happened. Grandpa and uncle are sick in the brain so if you ever see them do not sit on their lap or go anywhere with them if they ask." Boundary is not a word we use in the culture and it is a European term. However, it can still help in facilitating conversation. We can draw a picture of ourselves and our kids and draw a circle around their body and teach them that inside the circle is her bubble and her personal space that only few people can enter. We can begin to identify safe and non-safe people and who can enter or stay out. We need to teach our kids that they can kiss some family on the cheek, some they can shake hands and they should not sit on anyone's lap unless parents state it is ok. The child ought to have the right to just say hi and have no physical contact and not be pressured by family to kiss or hug them.

These conversations may decrease abuse because they will not be easy to target. It will create a space to talk openly with kids and teach them about their value, worth, and empower them to speak up about what happens in their bubble.

PROTECTING THE ABUSED CHILDREN

Tavris (1992) alerts us to the specific paradox faced by incest victims in America who endure abuse by those on whom they depend for the most basic psychological and physical care. The child must find a way to preserve a sense of trust in people who are untrustworthy, to preserve safety in a situation that is unsafe, control in a situation that is terrifying and unpredictable, and power in a situation that engenders helplessness. Unable to take care of herself, she must compensate for the failure of adult care and protection with the only means at her disposal, an immature system of psychological defenses. One defense is denial.

Children have tremendous respect for the elders and are raised to be respectful. They intuitively know to keep quiet and since incest occurs in secret, the message is given that it is not something you talk about. Therefore, kids will not share it unless parents have taught them to share and that secrets are never to be kept. Child molesters take time in choosing and deciding who to molest and they choose kids who are vulnerable, whose parents are not paying close attention, whose parents are absent or accommodating, kids who hold the label of liar, kids who are shy, etc.

FOCUS ON CHILDREN'S BODY LANGUAGE

Adults need to begin to pay attention to their children and notice the signs and not minimize them, but be curious and ask questions, "Why are you afraid? Did someone hurt you? You can tell me anything and I will never be mad at you for telling the truth, you should never keep secrets from me because my job is to protect you and if you keep secrets, I will not be able to keep you safe." "If anyone touches your private parts, your job is to tell mama." "Why are you afraid of him/her? You are my princess and my job is to make sure no one hurts you." If your child begins to excessively masturbate and is fixated in her/his private parts, it is normal and expected that you take her in her room and talk to her about private parts and make inquiries. If they suddenly become afraid to bathe, have nightmares, or are frightened, it is a parent's responsibility to sit with the child and explore the causes of the fear with loving and gentle questions. "I am sorry that you got scared. Come here and I want you to tell me all about what is so scary. The job of mama is to protect their kids and my job is to protect you, keep you safe and happy and your job is to tell me when you feel sad, scary, hurt and when someone does something to make you sad, scared or if they want you to keep a secret. Secrets have to be told to mama always. Did someone touch you in ways you did not like and in ways that you did like?" If no one intervenes, these beautiful helpless children are lost and leads to the creation of another generation of abused children.

UNDERSTANDING A CHILD'S VIEW

In order for a child to have survived trauma, she had to distrust her instinct that she was being harmed because the abuser was also the nurturer and protector.

She needs to keep her abuser in the role of her protector; therefore, she convinces herself that nothing bad is happening. When reality is too painful for a child, she moves her thinking into a fantasy world where the perpetrator is good. She begins to make excuses by minimizing, rationalizing and taking the blame on herself for the abuse in order to make some sense of it in her mind. This victim viewpoint from childhood is now keeping her from remembering the abuse as an adult and blocks her ability or instinct to protect her own child. She does not see the perpetrator as a danger and has a relationship with him as if nothing ever happened and will ultimately trust him to care for her child and another generation of incest continues. For this reason, it is imperative that adults intervene and correct this perception and help the child to avoid internalization and foster healing. For an adult to step in and protect the child is what will make the difference between surviving or suffering an emotional death.

PERSONAL EXAMPLE

For instance, it took a long time in psychotherapy for me to be able to change the above perspective. Because I wanted my family's acceptance and protection, I minimized the abuse and tried to paint a nicer picture and minimize one of my molester's actions. Later, I had clear evidence of the violation, but because I wanted to preserve that relationship I denied it to myself and was forced to address it when I became a mother. I knew I had to break the cycle and provide my children with a safe and loving environment that they can trust and depend on. My advice to mothers is, keep the molester far from your children and begin teaching your 2-year-olds about their body parts and that secrets are wrong. Parents do not have the luxury of hoping nothing bad happen; we have a responsibility to remove the molesters from our homes to ensure the protection of our children.

PROTECTION AND AN APOLOGY TO VICTIMS/SURVIVORS

To all the girls and boys whose bodies were violated, whose tears continue to flood rivers, and who have buried those feelings so deep they have minimal access to them: you are not alone. Things can get better. You do not have to use your beautiful body to get attention; you do not have to endure abuse from men and women. You do not have to numb your feelings with substances to cope; you do not have to carry their secrets and shame. You can choose differently. Tell someone you trust who will help you. Your presence is more powerful than your past. The worst is over. It is time to let go of the secrets that hold you captive and share your stories, if not with another person, in a journal. It is time to begin giving your body the respect it deserves. You can control your thoughts, your actions and decrease the pain by dealing with them in a constructive and healthy way. You have survived. You need to stand in front of a mirror and see yourself with eyes of possibilities, not what was taken. See your potential and abilities, see your beauty, see your kindness and see a bright and happy future.

Parents have the responsibility to begin talking to their children, apologize for not protecting them and create space to have a conversation without blaming. The time is now to help survivors overcome this trauma with love and support and for the family to provide love and understanding. It may be necessary to seek psychotherapy or spiritual assistance to help all the family involved heal and decide the best course of action to feel safe again.

PERSONAL EXAMPLE

If I had to do my adolescence over, I probably would be as afraid and probably keep quiet and pretend to be happy because it is easier to suffer in silence with your family than to share your pain and lose your family. Cutting family ties is unacceptable in our culture and family, as dysfunctional as it may be, will be there when you need them. The Cabo Verdean family is very loving and supportive and a teen will always sacrifice herself to protect the family. How can you cut off your source of strength, identity and protection? The best way for me was to ignore the harm and focus on the good. I denied any harm was being done while my invisible wounds bled. I had problems with self-love because I thought that love had a prize and my body was the cost. However, another part of me would have liked to break the silence and deal with the consequences. I would have liked to scream, "I will not dance with you anymore! Leave my room, and stop touching me!" "I would have liked to tell a teacher and be placed in the foster system and get help sooner. But most of all, I would have loved to have someone seen the pain and protected me. Do not get me wrong; I had friends and a lot of family members who were great and I have several wonderful memories. But I had no adult I trusted to share this pain with believing that they would protect me. Let us become the nurturing and trusting adults in whom a child will find protection, acceptance and shelter.

Today, I tell you, you are not alone and I pray my story gives you some support and helps you realize your inner strength. This was not your fault. It is not your responsibility to hold his shame. You have options and you decide which way you choose; there is no right or wrong way. It is what you can do given your current situation. For me, I knew that I had to endure this throughout my adolescence, but that as an adult I would have more choices and I could leave.

ADULT SURVIVORS CLAIMING THEIR HEALING

Cabo Verdean women have to start to understand the severe destruction that incest has caused on the individual and that this person walks and breathes, but feels empty inside. As an adult, it is a time for total independency while most survivors are severely handicapped. Some find themselves in unhealthy and abusive intimate relationships due to low self-worth and damaged goods mentality, severely depressed yet holding fulltime employment and raising a family with or without a supportive spouse or partner. That is when the full damage of childhood incest shows its full destruction on the body, mind and soul of an adult crippled with fear, insecurities and shame. However, she continues to present a façade to the world and herself that she is doing well.

The adult survivor has internalized the pain and is trying to superficially be strong when she is barely holding on. Instead of lending a hand, we are tearing her down with our words that in reality reflect the condition of our own heart. Don Miguel Ruiz wrote in his book The Four Agreements, "Nothing anyone says about you positive or negative is ever about you. It is always about the conditions of their heart." Let us unite as a community of strong, resilient women and begin a holistic change and cleanse our hearts of bitterness, envy, rage and begin the process of supporting each other to create a safe, nurturing and loving environment for all to truly live.

This environment of support is essential for all adults to start healing by recognizing that for the community as it currently operates, no one is coming to help you, to believe you or to lend you a hand. As an adult, you have to take the responsibility to seek supportive environments where that inner child can heal and you can heal along with her and start to love yourself for the first time in a long time. Start to demand respect from your environment. Start to set boundaries without guilt. Start to experience your worth without shame. Start to see the strength and courage that are buried under community lies and put downs. Begin to exercise your voice and say NO for the first time in a long time. End distractive and unhealthy relationships. Recognizing you are beautiful, worthy and no longer a door mat. You were beautifully made and your worth was not destroyed by the abuse; it was made greater and shines brighter in spite of it. For this healing to occur, adult survivors need to make some difficult changes.

Some suggestions are listed below:

1. Stop denying the abuse.

2. Face it, talk about it.

3. Be compassionate and kind to yourself.

4. Make self-care a priority.

5. Surround yourself with positive and supportive people.

6. Remove toxic people from your inner circle.

7. Remove the molester from your home, if it is possible.

8. By protecting your child, you will heal the wounded child within.

9. By being a better mother, your need for a mother's protection will decrease.

10. Join support groups that targets your struggles.

11. Start a Cabo Verdean women's support group.

Sisters and brothers, I cry with you and stand by your side in your suffering. I feel your agony in an untrustworthy community. I feel your rage in a huge family with no one home to listen or protect. I cry with you in your loneliness. I internally scream with you in a family where you have become the liar and the problem. I pray with you for strength to overcome and stand strong. It is past time you stand strong and decide that **NO LONGER WILL YOUR PAST DICTATE YOUR FUTURE.** It is time to stand strong as a survivor and no longer allow your body or mind to be used, misused or disrespected. It is past time to demand respect, faithfulness and devotion from your mate and respect from your family. It is time to see the Queen in you and demand Queen treatment. I see your beauty and strength; I see your courage and hidden abilities. I see you, pure, perfectly made, and washed clean by God of all past wounds.

PERSONAL EXAMPLE

I blamed myself for not saying no enough, for being too complacent, for not fighting. These were my attempts to understand this horrible situation without blaming my protector who became my violator. For survivors, children need to see them as good in order to cope and survive and the harm is that internalizing the blame may last a lifetime. I was left alone, and as an adult, that desire for nurturance and protection remains. I like most, developed a fake presentation of happiness and a great sense of humor as I faced my molesters daily. I acted like the betrayal, disrespect, and the ultimate violation of my body never occurred. As an adult, you now have the power and option to change your thinking and choose a healthier way to be.

The great news is that we have all it takes inside each one of us to transform the pain of the past to present triumph. It begins and ends with changing our thinking, which in turn changes our actions and turn to our faith.

CHAPTER 9

HEALING

Wounds have Healed
Night terrors ceased
Broken wings mended
Voice activated
Garden destroyed
Victim no longer
Enjoying the sunset
Witnessing the sunrise
Blessed by all the possibility it brings

"HE HEALS THE BROKENHEARTED AND BINDS UP THEIR WOUNDS."
– Psalms 147:3

There is difficulty in dealing with incest because both the victim and molester are part of the family. However, this violation makes it difficult to maintain a family unit by avoiding the topic. Incest creates an invisible monster that keeps eating at the soul of the victim daily and it worsens when it is ignored.

It is not easy to heal from incest, but it is possible to have the pain transform into something beautiful. I did it and so will you. No child is ever to blame for sexual abuse. Yes, we do blame ourselves for many reasons and at so many levels, but the reality is you are not to blame and no matter what you did or did not do, you are not to blame. You were a child that was used for sexual pleasure by an adult that should have protected you. It is crucial that you forgive yourself. Once you accept and forgive yourself, you can begin to be compassionate and loving with yourself. Treat yourself with the same kindness and gentleness you would treat a flower. See its beauty, strength and its delicateness. Nurture it, water it and see it blossoming. Give yourself all that you need to blossom. Offer pure water, excellent soil for growth, protection from unfriendly weather and a transformation is in process.

BREAK THE SILENCE, SECRETS NO MORE

Breaking the silence will most likely destroy the family support system. You may become the problem and some may abandon you to keep their facade intact. I say it has to be done for one important reason, to protect the girl in your tummy, the daughter next to you, your cousins, nieces, granddaughters, and all the beautiful girls in the family who he will surely molest as you were molested. Protecting them from that violation, intrusion, and sadness is worth doing at any cost. Isn't your baby girl's happiness more important than family security and support? Of course! Isn't her innocence worth you leaving your security? Of course! Isn't her smile worth it? Of course! Because of fear, are you going to do what your mother did? Are you going to pretend nothing is going on as he takes your child downstairs to play or takes her for a ride or to get ice cream? Are you going to look away as her innocent smile and love for life disappear to be replaced by pain and darkness? Think back to when no one protected you – is that the inheritance you want to pass on?

It is time to break the cycle and give our children the happiness we were robbed of. I know what I am asking is very difficult and it goes against the fabric of our culture and upbringing. We are a loving people who respect our elders and put family first. We depend on them and them on us. I know the pain it will cost to end relationships, and some of you may choose to stay connected and that is your decision. I am not here to judge. We do enough of it by ourselves. Some are not ready; they may be too scared, in severe denial of their own sexual abuse or in a living situation that depends on the molester.

The decisions to cut contact with some of my family members were easy once I realized the danger I would put my kids in otherwise. The most difficult part is living with that decision. For me, it is as if my heart was torn to pieces. It was clear why I kept quiet because it is so much easier to overlook, minimize than to become the one the family believes causes the pain. I did not want to be ostracized, the one no one calls, the one forgotten and blamed, the one who no longer has a place at any table. I felt crushed and rejected while the molesters believe they did nothing wrong and remained loved and protected by the family who continued to provide a place at the table for them.

I imagine how easy it would have been to keep quiet and pretend there were no molesters and have my family in my life. However, the price was too high for the mother in me. Victims and survivors, I understand the cost of telling the truth. I am not advising you to do it. However, I hope that as a community we change the perspective and shift protection to the victims/survivors and empower them to tell their truths without the possibility of losing a place at the table. Let us empower our survivors with the assurance that they will not be scapegoated; let us reassure them that under no circumstances would we protect the molesters over them; let us become vessels of healing and become salt to flavor their hope and be the light to guide them to wholeness. If our women and children believe we will support and protect them, they will have no problems breaking the silence.

I am sharing my process to help you consider all options and make a decision that works for you. I felt a deep sadness at losing some of my family whom I did not want to lose but lost anyway, sadness for the good memories, sadness for letting go of a piece of my soul and identity, and sadness for their inability to recognize my pain. The feeling of nostalgia remains as I think about them. Part of me will always miss them and wish things were different. However, when I look at my children's innocence, it makes it all worth it. I will make sure my kids inherit all the amazing cultural richness. They will learn our cultural compassion and ability to love and forgive. They will learn the value of family and respect for the elders. They will visit our country and learn all the richness it has to offer. I have not lost my connection to my culture, just a place at the family table. My hope and dream are that future generations experience unconditional acceptance and not be placed in a position to choose.

ACCEPTANCE

Realize that the image we have of family is a fictionalized fantasy needed to survive as a child. The reality is that those we love have inflicted permanent terror and destroyed our innocence and betrayed our trust. Realize that yes, they possess good qualities and bad ones too. We need to see the poisonous snake in them and in their actions clearly and never again allow the good in them to shadow the terror, poison, torment and pain they can spread. We need to say, "I was abused" rather than excuse or minimize the trauma in order to save the next generation.

We have to acknowledge the trauma in our past and talk about it or write about it and allow ourselves to feel what we feel without judgment or criticism. You may need to talk to someone you trust and share your story in order to protect the next generation and to help you heal. That has to be done with support and love. Once you accept your own history, you can become protective of your children, appropriately reading the signs of danger and also beginning to enjoy a healthy intimate relationship and so much more. We have to challenge the culture to shift the focus to protecting the child and hold the molesters accountable.

FINDING HIGHER POWER

Religious involvement serves as a unique strength for Cabo Verdeans coping with difficult experiences. Since religious institutions are important for many Cabo Verdeans, mental health agencies can collaborate with religious institutions in providing incest prevention and recovery programs.

Connecting with God or your individual higher power will help you heal and have a fundamental change. When my personal relationship with God was developed and strengthened, I began to see my worth in a different light. The darkness incest introduced was transformed by God's healing and love. Prayers and reading the bible and discovering my identity in God's words and promises have given me a new identity and has freed me from the past trauma. "Greater is he that is in you that he that is in the world."

Priscilla Shirer in her book <u>The Armor of God</u> presents a set of lists describing "My inheritance and identity in Christ." These lists have changed my life by allowing me to deepen my identity in how Jesus sees me and his power to heal.

CHALLENGE THE COMMUNAL CULTURAL VIEW

One common reason women state they keep quiet is to protect the perpetrator's family back in Cabo Verde that he is financially supporting from America. My response is he should have thought of that before committing a crime. If he wants to take care of his family, then he needs to keep his hands away from the children. The communal ideals are great, but what happens to accountability? Because he feeds his children, my child has to be the sacrificial lamb? Is the financial survival of his family more important than the emotional and spiritual survival of my child? Money for his child and horror for my child. He is harming my child in the worst way, but I have to protect his child and family so the community can say how wonderful I am?

Some may say that I am not honoring my culture's communal view. I love my culture and my people, but I refuse to sacrifice any one child for the well-being of a group. Because of this view, we have multiple generations of women who are corpses walking, breathing, and eating, but not living. The cost has been too high and it has to change. Why do we need to sacrifice the innocent? Let us start calling the police and have the child molesters arrested or tell them they are not welcome in our homes. Remove the shame and blame from our innocent kids and give them our love and reassure them that steps have been taken to secure their safety. If we are not willing or capable to protect our children, then I suggest that we consider not having children because it is a crime to give birth to an innocent, pure, dependent and beautiful child full of potential and abilities and then knowingly hand her over to your husband, father or uncle to molest because they have done the same to you or someone you know. Why is it so difficult to show our innocent children the support we are capable of? Why do we fail them when they most need our understanding, protection, love and unconditional support? We have to accept that there is a huge problem and spend our energy in healing, supporting and listening to each other's stories seriously, not smiling, joking or minimizing the issue. Accept and face the pain, the love, the hatred, the hope, the shattered life, and make invisible pain endured visible. Acknowledge and accept the harm done, which is very difficult to do because it means destroying the illusions of a loving family we have adopted as a child in order to survive the trauma. It is so much easier to pretend all is well than to shake and destroy these dysfunctional, but enduring long standing systems.

STOP MINIMIZING

We often excuse perpetrators' behavior in order not to face our pain and to keep the family intact. We say "the family member is no longer molesting me because maybe he is better. We have a wonderful time together, they are supportive and loving, and even the molester is kind to me and my kids. So what is the problem? Why destroy this happy home with my truth? Why not keep going and stay with my family support? Why not leave it in the past and keep being happy with this family that would help me financially and never asks for payment back? Why destroy the family who comes to my home every month and helps me in any way I need? Why destroy the molester who is married with kids and is very nice to me and my family? Why destroy a family that was here last week to fix the pipe and charge me nothing? Why destroy my loving and kind supports? When I had an accident, all the family came and took care of everything and we had such a wonderful time. Why take all that away, for what? Why bring up the past when no one will believe me anyway? Why become the cause for family disharmony? Why become the one blamed for breaking the family? What will I do if I cannot rely on them for support? I am not strong enough, I cannot do it. He is not molesting anyone else. Let's forgive, forget and live in peace, and I keep my support system intact. I do not even think about it anymore." These statements help us stay strong and connected, but this behavior nurtures the molester and empowers them to continue to use our children for their sexual satisfaction. The question remains, what is our next step? Do we unite and remove the fear victims have, or do we continue to foster and provide kids for the molester to destroy? Can we change the community to have a permanent place at the table for the girls and remove the plates of the child molesters?

CHANGE THE FAMILY RELATIONSHIPS

Another necessary step towards healing is to change the relationship you have with the family and the molester. You have to see them in their entirety and make some choices. How do you want the relationship to change depends on what works for you. How much contact and how are you going to protect your child? First, you have to tell your story because it is healing to share and break the silence. You decide which family members are supportive and believe you, and those will be your support system. Second, you have to decide if you will remain in contact with the molester or not, and if you plan to keep contact, what is your action plan to keep your kids safe with the awareness that if he is with them he will molest them. Third, you decide how you will remain in contact and protect yourself from those family members who will put you down and disrespect you with their words.

One element of the richness of my Cabo Verdean heritage is that we welcome all into our homes and we extend help to all from the community who need it. My step-mother and father were exemplary for this. They always accommodated extended family and strangers in their home. They let people stay at their home rent free while they worked to assist family back home. They were provided with everything and treated as part of the family without any expectation. I liked this when I was growing up. However, very few of these people returned to show gratitude, which was a lesson for me. This hospitality is a great ability of the culture to help each other, but it puts a burden on the family to accommodate others without an option to choose an alternative. It also puts the girls at home in danger of being sexually abused.

I am very careful now as to who enters my home for the protection of my children and this is mostly due to my husband's incredible ability to set limits and put his kids first. He is my center and my family's greatest protector. Even though, I like the idea of helping the community, but not at the expense of harming my family.

STRENGTHEN YOUR SUPPORT SYSTEM

We need to build a support network and practice new ways of taking care of ourselves. I have been blessed with wonderful friends that have become part of my family. The people that come to my home are people that I trust and if I have any doubt, they do not come to my home. God placed many people in my path to assist and help me as I endured years of sexual abuse, neglect, feeling abandoned and unwanted. These are the people who water my seed with support and encouragement. I believe if you were to take some time, you will locate similar supportive people in your life.

I am blessed and I truly believe you can also have a complete and fulfilled life. However, to achieve this fulfillment, you have to be honest and know who supports you and surround yourself with people who will help you heal. Sadly, the people who help you heal may not be your family of origin.

We need people in our lives that will help us heal, not cause more harm. Our thoughts are like seeds, and if the seeds are watered with dirty water, meaning statements like, "You cannot associate with my kids, you are bad news. You wanted him, you asked for it, it was your fault, you are a liar." These messages will grow into a tree of negativity and condemnation. However, to heal, you need to start watering your seeds with pure water and good fertilizer, which includes positive words, words of praise, encouragement like; "You are beautiful, you are strong, I am so sorry he did that to you, you are not to blame, I love you, you will get through this, you are not alone, I will always stand by you, whatever you need please call me." That is how you begin to change the negative messages you have received and surround yourself with people who will help you grow in a positive direction.

My focus today is not on the hell endured, but the strength I gained from it and the blessings God placed on my path as I endured. You are not alone. You may feel alone, unprotected and lost in pain, but remember God is always with you. Trust him and he will find a way. Trust the power within you and regain control of your life. Focus on your present and remove the obstacles preventing you from being happy, fulfilled and whole.

My beautiful and courageous and powerful sisters and brothers, I pray this book awakens in you the courage that is dormant. I pray you recognize your internal power and abilities and let your light shine brightly never to be dimmed or blown out. You are resilient, from a culture of tremendous strength and capacity to overcome adversity. All of these strengths are living and breathing inside of you.

Healing is an individual process and will look different for everyone. There is an intense desire to feel well quickly and individuals can feel that the process is taking too long or they are not doing it "right." Healing is not defined by a complete absence of thoughts or feelings about a traumatic experience, but rather being able to live with it in a way where it is not in control of your life. It is important to be gentle, patient and compassionate with yourself as you move through this healing process and the trauma becomes integrated into your life story, but it is not the only story.

CHAPTER 10
COMMUNITY RESPONSIBILITY

Wake Up
Pain weaving threads of wholeness and beauty
Wakening dormant power
Stirring heart and soul for a new identity
Survivor of horror enlightened by courage
Yesterday's pain is dismantled
Rejoicing has anchored

"FOR WITH GOD NOTHING WILL BE IMPOSSIBLE."
– Luke 1:37

Recently, on January 16, 2018, the government of Cabo Verde announced a plan to combat sexual violence against children; the plan will include a country-wide notification system. I was pleased to hear this news, but we have a long journey ahead. Long before such recent attempts to raise awareness of this issue, I embarked on a humble journey to sound an alarm about this crisis in our beloved Cabo Verdean community both in the U.S. and in Cabo Verde. This book concentrates on the Cabo Verdean community because, whereas most cultures are able to talk about it and have understood its detrimental effects, much of our (Cabo Verdean) population – in particular the most rural, impoverished and less educated – remains in denial. Many often make excuses, minimize and deny its existence. This section will provide some suggestions to shift the community to protect the girls and boys from sexual abuse.

ZERO TOLERANCE FOR INCEST

It is time to begin to talk openly about this taboo and begin creating a community where this type of behavior is not tolerated. We all know who the child molesters are in our families so let us break the silence by considering calling the reporting agency when they abuse children. Let us tell them they are not welcomed in our homes instead of praying they do not touch our children, or denying that they will abuse. The reality is, if they are around children, they will molest them. Do not kid yourselves; children are being molested.

Are we ready to change? Are we seeing the damage incest does? Can we support each other? This change cannot be achieved alone. We need each other. Are we ready to end this vicious cycle of abuse? When will it end? When will we have peace? When will we heal and have no need to medicate our headaches? When will we speak the truth consequences be darned? When will we protect the next generations? When will we hold the perpetrators accountable? When will we call the police on them? When will we choose our children instead of our husbands? When will we get our voices back?

Let us begin today. Let us say no more sexual abuse, no more put downs, no more disrespect, and no more gossip. Let us say yes to empowerment, yes to unity, yes to support, and yes to encouragement and growth.

REPORT THE MOLESTERS

It is our responsibility to begin reporting child molesters to authorities because incarceration may be the only cure. I am acutely aware that none of us want to involve the authorities, but the reality is that the molesters are the ones who broke the law, thus involving the police not us. They are the ones who seduce with their kindness in daylight, but at night destroy, rape, violate, and make childhoods disappears. The molesters brought this response on themselves. For me, when I was strong enough to call and report the molesters, the statute of limitations had expired and so I could not report them. The statute of limitations is 15 years after the abuse. However, policymakers are considering extending the timeframe, but this change has not yet occurred. Perpetrators continue abusing children because we give them access to our children. America has specific laws in place to protect children from perpetrators because they are a danger, and the Cabo Verdean community needs to start recognizing the danger as well. By reporting the perpetrators, we are assuring the safety of many children.

FEMALES TAKE A STAND TO PROTECT THE VICTIMS

I am calling on women to take a stand and make a commitment to protect all the children in their families. You already know the molesters in your family so educate the young girls about them, call Child Protective Services, or the police. I guarantee you he has and will continue to molest. Have someone else call in the report if you do not feel safe to do it. The report can also be done anonymously. Most families usually have an outspoken member who can use their power to help those who are unable to voice their own pain. This reporting is one way to begin supporting the survivors. The responding agency needs to be educated about the culture and not believe the family's presentation because we all know how well we can present to others.

The women who were not sexually abused have a huge responsibility in helping young girls. Your strength and compassion are vital for their healing. Your strength is needed to help others by listening and not judging or denying their story. Be genuine in saying, "How can I help? What do you need? I am sorry? I am here for you." Provide hugs and encouragement, and be clear in holding the molester accountable. As painful or conflicting as it may be, choosing the child will lead to healing and wholeness.

I know many who have been molested who continue to minimize and deny it happened to them. However, you need to think about the other girls in the family growing up. The molester will move on to others once you are too old. It will never stop with you; it will continue until they die or go to jail. It is our responsibility to protect the next generation. Just imagine if someone had protected you, if someone had stopped him, or if someone had reported him, then you would never have been violated. I once heard someone say, "To remove pain from your heart and have peace, you have to remove the thorn causing pain in others' feet."

RESPECTABLE MALES TAKE A STAND TO PROTECT THE VICTIMS

It starts with men holding other men accountable and stopping the objectification of women. The danger is when women are seen as objects, then it is easy for them to be disrespected, abused and violated. Due to this view, we have created a generational problem that has been normalized.

There are many great men in the community who do not molest children nor approve of this behavior. Tacitly, they are also reinforcing the perpetrators by their silence, by ignoring it or by minimizing it. Therefore, it is very easy to keep the secret because no one wants to know and those who know ignore it. Again, the child is abandoned when the child most needs to be protected and provided with safety. Men, wake up, stand up, open your mouths, and become a voice of reason and protection for the innocent. Use your power and strength to lift the blame from our children. Do not allow the community to force a child to carry the sin of these men. Let us not force the innocent children to carry the cross of the communities' shame, blame, and guilt, and stand alone with this unbearable cross that was never theirs to own. Men, please protect the children and stand against this injustice and eliminate the power of the perpetrators.

Respectable men in our community, you need to become a protector to all females. How would your community change if you no longer allowed perpetrators to sexualize girls with their hands or suggestive comments. Start challenging and confronting perpetrators by providing them with guidance on the impact of their behavior. How about providing support and encouragement to mothers, and guidance and protection to girls? It is past time for your help to protect the children and women of the community.

CHILD MOLESTERS, YOUR DAYS OF ABUSE ARE OVER

Much love and understanding are available in the community for the abuser while the child being abused is ignored. The adult survivor tries to take a stand for her sanity and is confronted with hostility and rejection from the family. She is left with no options, often having to leave the family. The worst part is that the molesters do not believe they have a problem because the community protects them, and they will continue to molest girls in the family until they die. This protection is what breeds incest in the family. The more protection they get, the more dangerous they become beginning to feel untouchable and increasing their molestation of girls. Women have extensive excuses to protect the molesters: "He did not mean it. He was possessed by the devil, he was drunk, he confused you with his wife, he fell on his head when he was young, and he is like that so stay away. That is how men are, it's nothing." Until the molesters are held accountable, our beautiful girls will inherit the same violations you endured and denied, and have had to ignore to survive. It would be amazing if we could put the same effort into protecting the girls. Stop excusing the molester's behaviors. The truth is, it is inexcusable. Let us protect the innocent children and recognize their silent screams for help.

Molesters, I plead and challenge you to own your responsibility and recognize the permanent damage you inflict on innocent girls and how you continue to destroy and violate them. Do your best not to be around kids when you get sexual desires. If you are unable to control your urges, call someone you trust to talk with, get on your knees and ask God to help you and take this compulsion away. You are also loved by your creator. I believe you have the capacity to stop and with help you can stop. I encourage you to read about the impact of sexual abuse on the victim and recognize the silent pain your actions are causing. Your few minutes of pleasure will leave a life time of pain and suffering. STOP touching and violating kids because it is a crime! Children are not old enough to consent.

You need to realize that as a community we are no longer protecting you from the consequences of your action. You have two options: stop or go to jail. It is time you begin to think about your community and seek individual help.

CHALLENGE THE CULTURAL NORMS

As a culture, we do not talk about problems or offenses committed against us. We bury our pain alive and it crawls out of the grave and holds us as we ignore it or bury it again and gain. Often, people hide their hurt feelings for the well-being of others or for fear of not looking good to the public. We are a community that will hide our pain and pretend nothing is wrong and never confront a person who has harmed us to work it out. We excuse their behavior in our head and remain in relationship with them no matter how much pain it causes. Often, we feel we have no choice. However, we do have a choice: we might choose to do nothing and suffer in silence because it is easier than confronting and risk being ostracized. Second, our community needs to learn to focus on protecting the girls and work on abolishing the objectification of women and demand respect from our brothers, fathers, uncles, grandfathers and cousins. Third, we need to stop protecting the molesters and hold them accountable for sexually abusing children, and stop excusing their behavior.

I believe we have to educate and provide the community with the tools necessary to handle this assault in ways that the child victim is protected and provide encouragement to move into a more healing position. Once awareness is in place, then we need to move forward to where other cultures are at handling this problem. There is more attention paid to this issue in Cabo Verde. However, the Cabo Verdeans residing in the U.S. are not moving with the changes occurring in their birth country or their adopted one. Most are frozen in the time that they immigrated and holding on tightly to the good values while perpetuating the destructive behavior.

COMMUNITY CHANGES

As a community, the time has come to start listening to the painful truth and genuinely heal ourselves and help others. Let us start by seeing the tears of shame and blame, seeing the tears of self-hatred and fears, seeing the tears of betrayal, seeing the tears of invisible wounds and innocence lost, seeing the tears of lowliness and isolation, seeing the tears of forgiveness and letting go, seeing the tears of confronting and accepting, seeing the tears of courage and exposure, seeing the tears of removing the shackles, seeing the tears of healing and wholeness, and seeing the tears of shame decreasing.

The community sees incest as non-exploitive. This adaptation formation is to deal with the molestation as best they can. Denying molestation and incest is the best way the community knows how to cope and survive. They do not consider how incest affects the victims; rather, the priority is how it could affect the community both here in America and in Cabo Verde. If the perpetrator is supporting family in America and in Cabo Verde, disclosing incest would have a transnational economic impact. For instance, the family in Cabo Verde relies on assistance from families in America, and if the perpetrator goes to jail, there would be no one to care for the family in Cabo Verde or at home. In addition, the family name would be brought under scrutiny, which would cause the victim to lose her virtue and have no hope of a future. For these reasons, the culture believes the best way of handling incest is to do nothing. The victims/survivors ignore their pain and adapt to a false sense of contentment and mental health while hiding internal turmoil.

The community continues to function as if nothing has happened. The mother cannot afford to split the family and the family cannot afford to share this secret outside the community. In the most loving family when incest occurred, the best way to continue functioning is to pretend nothing has happened. If they were to see incest as exploitive, then the systems in place would not be effective. As long as incest is seen as non-exploitive, the victims have no choice but to appear unaffected by incest and act as if nothing is wrong, which increases and intensifies the belief that it is non-exploitive. However, this view is far from the truth. The impact is painful, multidimensional and often permanent.

You may recall back in Chapter 4 my interview with an 89-year-old woman who likened women to trees and men to saws. We cannot afford to continue being helpless however. Instead, we need to wake up the trees' dormant voices and abilities and uncover the generational secrets. Let the land breathe fresh air without holding on to past secrets. Witness the magical power of the forest as the trees and plants blossom, and witness all the fears, shame, pain and blame dissipate. Bring pure water and allow the trees to grow free of pain and fear for generations to come. The forest will bring forth new and dormant beauty, and trees will stretch their arms and allow light to penetrate and shine through bringing life back to the land. The forest will stand strong and protect its young and nurture them, and allow them to run free in the fields since the saw is no longer welcomed there. The forest has overcome, let joy and peace fill the land.

HOPE FOR THE FUTURE

It is time for this beautiful community filled with great people to join hands and create a garden filled with hope and fulfilled dreams. A new generation where no child will be left in the cold. It is time to have the molesters leave the garden and face the consequences of their actions. It is time to bring the victims/survivors back to the family fold with love and celebration. It is time to apologize and heal the survivors still in shackles. United we can heal.

It is time to start loving and protecting the innocent. If we remain passive, nothing will change and silence is not an option anymore. There have been too many generations of abuse, too many generations of feeling powerless, too many generations of denial. It is time to find our God given power and say the abuse ends today and now. Let us liberate ourselves and reclaim our maternal instincts to protect our children and stand up for ourselves and finally believe that we have the right to say no, no more, it ends today and now. We can definitely create a new world for our children and for ourselves.

Thank you for reading this book. To victims and survivors reading this book, I hope you have allowed some of the blame and shame to be shed off your bodies and minds and have started to recognize your greatness. I hope you develop a new positive thinking pattern filled with beauty and unlimited possibility, and I wish you healing, peace and joy.

A BLOOMING GARDEN

A Caboverdiana Woman
The unyielding roots planted in purity
She radiates hope and blossoms wildly
Beauty and strength unveiled by the peaceful wind
She wakes
The sun with fresh cuscus from hours of labor
She heals
The heart and soul of her community
She instills
Hope and courage to her people
She breastfeeds
The babies and raises a village
She stands powerfully
While she bleeds from the harsh environment
Her heavenly sun
Penetrates the darkness
She is called
Mother, grandmother, aunt, cousin, friend,
She is also called,
Provider, protector, defender, teacher, inventor and Poderoza
Her mind holds
Unlimited power and infinite oral traditions
She sings
The pain of immigration, separation, hopelessness and abuse
She rises
As ocean takes more loved ones to faraway lands
She eradicates
Garden of sacrificed children and adolescents
She is the volcanic eruption
That castrated the saw
She is the massacre
Of generational trauma and violence
She embodies unlimited power
She stands in God's light
She is a
Caboverdiana Woman

REFERENCES

Alexander, P.C. (1985). A systems theory conceptualization of incest. Family Process, 24, 79-88.

Bass, Ellen., & Laura Davis. (1988). The Courage to Heal. New York: Harper Collins.

Beezley, Mrazek, P. & Bentovin (1981). Definition and recognition of sexual abuse: Historical and cultural perspective. Sexually Abused Children and their Families (p. 5-16. New "York: Pergamon Press.

Blume, E. Sue. 1990. Secret Survivors: Uncovering Incest and its Effects in Women. New York, John Wiley and Sons.

Briere, John, Henschel & Smiljanich (1992). Methodological issues in the study of sexual abuse effects. Journal of Consulting and Clinical Psychology, 60 (2), 195-203.

Butler, Sandra. (1996). Conspiracy of Silence The Trauma of Incest. Volcano Press.

Butman, Richard E. (1983). Hidden Victims: the facts about incest 20-23.

Courtois, C.A. (1988). The incest experience and its aftermath. Victimology: An International Journal, 4, 337-347.

Dugan, Timothy., & Robert, Coles. (1989). The Children In Our Times: Studies in the Development of Resiliency. New York: Brunner/Mazel.

Finkelhor, David, & Hotaling, Stephanie. (1990). Sexual abuse in a national survey of adult man and women: Prevalence, characteristics and risk factors. Child Abuse and Neglect, 14 19-28.

Furniss, T. (1984). Family process in the treatment of intrafamilial child sexual abuse. Journal of Family Therapy, 5, 263-279.

Greenfield, Sidney (1976). In search of social identity: Strategies of Ethnic identity Management Amongst Cape Verdeans in southern Massachusetts. Luso-Brazilian Review, pp 3-19.

Giovanni, Jeanne., & Becerra, Rosina M. (1979). Defining child abuse. New York: Free Press.

Halter, Marilyn (1985). Between Race And Ethnicity. University of Illinois Press, Chicago, pp 3-185.

Human Rights Report (1998). Cabo Verde.

Lima-Neves, Terza Alice Silva (2015). *D'NOSMANE-Gender, Collective Identity and Leadership in the Cape Verdean Community in the United States.* Journal of Cape Verdean studies, 1(1), 57-82.

McIntyre, K. (1981). Role of mothers in father-daughter incest: A feminist analysis. Social Work, 26 463-466.

Miller, Deborah., & Pat Kelly. (1995). Coping with Incest. New York: The Rosen Publishing, Inc.

Monteiro, Joao. (1997). Reflections of Cape Verdeans Creoleness. Cimboa, pp.19-27.

Morrall, Lesley. (1988). Cross-Generational Incest: A Critical review of Literature. University Of South Africa.

O'Brien (1987). The effects of incest on female adolescent development.

O'Hare & Taylor K. (1983). The reality of incest. Women and Theory, 2, 214-230.

Pilgrim, Aminah. (2015). *"Free Men Name Themselves:"* U.S. Cape Verdeans &Black Identity Politics in the Era of Revolutions, *1955-75.* Journal of Cape Verdean Studies, 1 (1), 101-120.

Renvoize, J. (1982). Incest: A family pattern. London: Routledge and Hegan Paul.

Reposa, R.E. & Zuelzer, M.B. (1983). Family theory with incest. International Journal of family therapy, 6, 111-136.

Resende-Santos, Joao. (2015). Cape Verde and Its Diaspora: Economic Transnationalism and Homeland Development. Journal of Cape Verdean Studies, 2 (1), 69-107.

Russell, D.E.H. (1983). The incidence and prevalence of intrafamilial and extrafamilial sexual abuse of female children. Child Abuse and Neglect, 7, 133-147.

Russell, Diana, (1986). The Secret Trauma: Incest in the Lives of Girls and women. New York: Harper collins Publisher.

Russell, Diana. (1997). Behind Closed Doors in White South Africa. New York: St. Martin's Press.

Schultz, L.G. (1982). Child Sexual Abuse in historical perspective. Journal of Social Work and human Sexuality, 1, 22-36.

Serrano, A.C. & Gunzburger, D.W. (1983). An historical perspective of incest. International Journal of Family Therapy, 5 70-82.

Tavris, Carol. (1992). Between The Incest-Survivors Machine. New York:

Thornman, G. (1983). Incestuous Families. Illinois: Charles C. Thomas.

Triandis, Harry. (1980). Handbook of Cross-Cultural Psychology. Allyn and Bacon, Inc.

Wattenberg, E. (1985). In a different light: A feminist perspective on the role of mothers in father-daughter incest. Child Welfare, 65, 202-212.

Will, D. (1983). Approaching the incestuous and sexually abused family. Journal of Adolescence, 6 229-245.

RECOMMENDED READINGS FOR HEALING

BOOKS FOR PARENTS

Caring for Sexually Abused Children: A Handbook for Families & Churches, By R. Timothy Kearney.

Those are MY Private Parts, By Diane Hansen.

The Right Touch: A Read-Aloud Story to Help Prevent Child Sexual Abuse (Jody Bergsma Collection), By Sandy Kleven and Jody Bergsma.

BOOKS FOR CHILDREN

I Said No! A kid-to-kid guide to keeping your private parts private, By Kimberly King.

It's My Body (Children's Safety & Abuse Prevention) [Paperback].

BOOKS FOR ADOLESCENTS

How Long Does It Hurt: A Guide to Recovering from Incest and Sexual Abuse for Teenagers, Their Friends, and Their... By Cynthia L. Mather, Judy Wood, Eliana Gil and Kristina E. Debye.

In Their Own Words: A Sexual Abuse Workbook for Teenage Girls, By Karen Riskin and Lulie Munson.

All Grown Up And No Place To Go: Teenagers In Crisis (Revised Edition), By: David Elkind.

Invisible Girls: The Truth About Sexual Abuse--A Book for Teen Girls, Young Women, and Everyone Who Cares About Them, By Patti Feuereisen.

How Long Does It Hurt: A Guide to Recovering from Incest and Sexual Abuse for Teenagers, Their Friends, and Their Families, By Cynthia L. Mather.

It Happened to Me: A Teen's Guide to Overcoming Sexual Abuse (workbook), By William Lee Carter.

BOOKS FOR ADULTS

Outgrowing the Pain: A Book for and About Adults Abused as Children, By Eliana Gil.

The Courage to Heal Workbook, By Laura Davis.

The Courage to Heal (4th Edition).

A Guide for Women Survivors of Child Sexual Abuse (20th Anniversary Edition), By Ellen Bass.

The Sexual Healing Journey: A Guide for Survivors of Sexual Abuse (Revised Edition), By Wendy Maltz.

Incest and Sexuality: A Guide to Understanding and Healing, By Wendy Maltz.

No Secrets No Lies: How Black Families Can Heal from Sexual Abuse, By Robin D. Stone.

BOOKS FOR HUSBANDS AND PARTNERS

Allies in Healing: When the Person You Love Was Sexually Abused as a Child, By Laura Davis.

Ghosts in the Bedroom: A Guide for the Partners of Incest Survivors, By Ken Graber.

What About Me? A Guide for Men Helping Female Partners Deal with Childhood Sexual Abuse, By Grant Cameron.

CHRISTIAN READING
The Bible.

The Armor of God, By Priscilla Shirer.

Gideon: Your weakness. God's strength, By Priscilla Shirer.

ABOUT THE AUTHOR

Dr. Rosilda James is a wife and mother of two amazing children, a licensed psychologist, an advocate and an educator. She was born in Fogo, Cabo Verde and immigrated to Boston, Massachusetts at age 10. She earned a Bachelor of Arts in Psychology and Sociology from Bridgewater State University. She then moved to San Francisco, California where she earned a Masters in Marriage and Family Therapy from the University of San Francisco. She went on to earn a Masters and Doctorate in Clinical Psychology from The Wright Institute in Berkeley, California.

Dr. James has been with Kaiser Permanente since 2002 where she is currently a Hospital-Based Psychiatric Consultant. She also has a private practice where she treats couples, adults and families. She was an adjunct professor for 5 years at The Wright Institute in Berkeley.

90309505R00075

Made in the USA
Columbia, SC
02 March 2018